Interpersonal Conflict Resolution

Alan C. Filley

Interpersonal Conflict Resolution

Management Applications Series

Alan C. Filley, University of Wisconsin, Madison
Series Editor

Interpersonal Conflict Resolution

Alan C. Filley

University of Wisconsin, Madison

Scott, Foresman and Company   Glenview, Illinois

Dallas, Tex.   Oakland, N.J.   Palo Alto, Cal.   Tucker, Ga.

For those, like Florence,
who listen.

Library of Congress Catalog Number: 74-77512
ISBN: 0-673-07589-3

Foreword

The Management Applications Series is concerned with the application of contemporary research, theory, and techniques. There are many excellent books at advanced levels of knowledge, but there are few which address themselves to the application of such knowledge. The authors in this series are uniquely qualified for this purpose, since they are all scholars who have experience in implementing change in real organizations through the methods they write about.

Each book treats a single topic in depth. Where the choice is between presenting many approaches briefly or a single approach thoroughly, we have opted for the latter. Thus, after reading the book, the student or practitioner should know how to apply the methodology described.

Selection of topics for the series was guided by contemporary relevance to management practice, and by the availability of an author qualified as an expert, yet able to write at a basic level of understanding. No attempt is made to cover all management methods, nor is any sequence implied in the series, although the books do complement one another. For example, change methods might fit well with managing by objectives.

The books in this series may be used in several ways. They may be used to supplement textbooks in basic courses on management, organizational behavior, personnel, or industrial psychology/sociology. Students appreciate the fact that the material is immediately applicable. Practicing managers will want to use individual books to increase their skills, either through self study or in connection with management development programs, inside or outside the organization.

Alan C. Filley

Preface

The opposite of conflict is problem solving. Conflict generally ends in loss; problem solving, on the other hand, ends in the satisfactory achievement of the needs of the involved parties. If this book is successful, readers will learn how to engage in problem solving and how to change conflict situations into problem-solving situations.

Two values associated with problem solving are that it can result in objectively superior decisions to those resulting from typical conflict methods and that it can make the involved parties feel like winners. Without making any moral judgments, people who feel like winners will have more energy, creativity, and measured intelligence than the same people who feel like losers.

Eric Berne has said, "We are all born princes and princesses, and our parents turn us into frogs." If this book is successful, readers will know why this is true and, perhaps, will be in a position to help turn frogs back into princes and princesses.

No specific educational background or technical knowledge is necessary to understand this book, though material is drawn from current research and theory on conflict resolution in the behavioral sciences. Chapters 1 and 2 analyze the conflict process and the various ways in which conflicts can be resolved. Next, Chapters 3-6 explain the effects of language, personal behavior, attitudes, and organization on the achievement of different interpersonal outcomes. Chapters 7 and 8 describe the Integrative Decision Making method of problem solving in detail. Finally, Chapter 9 discusses the conditions associated with changes in personal behavior so as to stimulate the use of and success with problem-solving methods.

A series of exercises demonstrating issues and behaviors discussed in the text is included in the appendix; appropriate exercises are referred to the reader's attention at the end of most chapters. While in one sense the book may be read without the use of the exercises, maximum learning can only be achieved through their use. This book is in some sense a manual for people who are working in groups.

The Integrative Decision Method described in detail in Chapters 7 and 8 has been used in a variety of organizations including private businesses, government agencies, labor unions, families, and universities. The focus of application is upon conflicts or problem solving between individuals or small groups. International conflicts or difficulties between broad social groups are not included. The book can show you how to solve disagreements with your spouse, business partner, or subordinate; it cannot tell you how to solve the tension in the Middle East.

As will be evident, a number of people and ideas have shaped the content of this book. In particular, I have benefited from the work of Norman R. F. Maier at the University of Michigan; I have never met him but have gained immensely from his research, insights, and excellent exercises. Others who have contributed in some way are Milan Mockovak, Larry Cummings, Florence Filley, Robert House, R. Shukla, and Megan Partch.

Alan C. Filley

Contents

Types and Sources of Conflict

1

As humans we live our lives within a web of social relationships, most of which seem almost mechanical in their predictability and smoothness of function. We seek, establish, and maintain predictable patterns in our lives to avoid the anxiety of the unpredictable; such patterns, once established, require little conscious choice as they operate. We have predictable patterns for interacting with our family, for going to work in the morning, for performing in a job, for shopping at the market, and for socializing with others. Yet, because we are not solely mechanical, because we are social creatures in a social system, these patterns are not absolutely predictable.

We must also reckon with the elements of chance. While we can predict the movement of the solar system with relative certainty, we can only speak of the likelihood or probability of driving to work or of greeting the guard at the entrance. An accident or illness may have occurred to alter our usual routines. Finally, as human animals, we introduce a third element into our social systems, that of freedom (Boulding, 1964). We are capable of planning, of holding in our minds some picture of the future, and of altering our usual patterns of behavior.

Within our various social relationships are some which involve real or perceived differences between two or more parties. Where the interests of the parties are mutually exclusive—that is, where the gain of one party's goal is at the cost of the other's, or where the parties have

1

different values—then the resulting social interaction between the parties contains fertile ground for conflict.

It is our freedom which allows us to learn about our own social systems. We are able (1) to discover those elements of our systems which increase the likelihood of conflict, (2) to develop contingency plans when chance occurrences create disruptions, and (3) to produce and to improve systems for resolving conflict which maximize the benefits and minimize the costs to the parties involved. In this first chapter we shall be concerned with those characteristics of a system which increase the likelihood of conflict and with the system of conflict production. Such discussion permits us to organize in ways which minimize conflict, if that is the desired goal. Furthermore, by knowing the natural system of conflict production, we may adjust actions or conditions before conflicts take place, rather than wait for conflicts to develop before taking action.

In later chapters we shall focus on the conflict resolution process. Either because it may not be useful to avoid conflicts or because conflict develops as an unanticipated outcome, the resolution of conflict becomes necessary. We shall examine the various systems of resolution and suggest how they may be applied.

KINDS OF CONFLICT

Not all conflicts are of the same kind. Some, for example, follow definite rules and are not typically associated with angry feelings on the part of the parties, while others involve irrational behavior and the use of violent or disruptive acts by the parties. As a first step, therefore, we shall distinguish between conflicts which are *competitive* and those which are *disruptive*. In competitive situations there can be a victory for one party only at the cost of the opponent's total loss and the way in which the parties relate to each other is governed by a set of rules. The parties strive for goals which are mutually incompatible. The emphasis of each party is upon the event of winning, rather than upon the defeat or reduction of the opponent. The actions of each party are selected using criteria based on the probability of leading to successful outcomes, and the competition terminates when the result is obvious to both sides (Rapoport, 1960).

In the disruptive conflict, on the other hand, the parties do not follow a mutually acceptable set of rules and are not primarily concerned with winning. Instead, they are intent upon reducing, defeating, harming, or driving away the opponent. The means used are expedient, and the atmosphere is one of stress, anger, or fear. In extreme cases, the parties in disruptive conflict will abandon rational behavior and behave in any manner necessary to bring about the desired outcome, the goal of defeat.

Experience tells us that conflicts are usually distributed along a continuum between those that are competitive and those that are disruptive. Anger arises in a game and causes disruption. A competitor changes his behavior from a rational pursuit of a strategy of winning to an irrational act of aggression. Thus, the motives of the parties and the degree of strategic control which each exhibits are important factors in determining the degree to which a conflict is competitive or disruptive.

For a further elaboration of the kinds of conflict, we may describe the interaction between the parties according to (1) their mutuality of interests and (2) their perception of resource availability. As seen in Table 1–1, when parties seek real or perceived scarce resources (for example, victory or a share of a fixed sum) and when they have a mutuality of interests, the relationship is one of competition. When they seek real or perceived scarce resources and have unlike interests, their relationship is likely to be characterized by fighting and disruption. When the parties seek abundant resources but have dissimilar interests, their interaction will contain disagreement. Finally, when the parties seek abundant resources and have similar interests, they will most probably resort to problem solving.

Competition, disruption, and disagreement all imply a win-lose outcome (or at least some degree of winning or losing by each of the parties). Problem solving, on the other hand, implies the development of an outcome which provides acceptable gain to both parties. Thus, if the focus of competition changes from a win-lose game to a situation involving enhancement of skill or knowledge by the parties, it becomes problem solving since the parties are now, in effect, asking each other, "How can we interact in a manner which increases the benefit to both of us?" Likewise, if opposing parties in a fight realize the mutuality of their interests and the existence of abundant resources or if debaters

TABLE 1–1.   Elements of Conflict.

	Like interests	Unlike interests
Seek scarce resources	Competition/games	Fights/disruption
Seek abundant resources	Problem solving	Disagreement/debate

change their emphasis from argument to the achievement of a correct solution, then their interactions will also shift to a problem-solving mode.

The point in this classification scheme is that conflict has been defined in terms of incompatible goals and different values, but that such differences are frequently *perceived rather than real.* If opposing parties can change their perceptions of resources from scarce to abundant and can recognize the mutuality of their interests, it is often possible to change from a form of conflict to a form of problem solving.

We may summarize the characteristics of a conflict situation as follows:

1) At least two parties (individuals or groups) are involved in some kind of interaction.

2) Mutually exclusive goals and/or mutually exclusive values exist, in fact or as perceived by the parties involved.

3) Interaction is characterized by behavior designed to defeat, reduce, or suppress the opponent or to gain a mutually designated victory.

4) The parties face each other with mutually opposing actions and counteractions.

5) Each party attempts to create an imbalance or relatively favored position of power vis-à-vis the other.

THE VALUES OF CONFLICT

Conflict, a social process which takes various forms and which has certain outcomes, itself is neither good nor bad. The conflict process merely leads to certain results, and the value of those results as favorable or unfavorable depends upon the measures used, the party making the judgment, and other subjective criteria. Let us consider some of the possible positive values of conflict:

The diffusion of more serious conflict

Competitive situations such as games provide conflict processes and outcomes which are governed by rules. These types of conflict seem to provide entertainment value and tension release to the parties. Winning and losing are identified as events and may have little effect on the self-perception of any player. That is, to lose in a competitive event does not suggest that an individual is less important, has less status, or is less valued as a person. In addition, in competitive situations aggressive behavior can be channeled along socially acceptable lines.

Viewed another way, conflict processes which are institutionalized (that is, for which acceptable resolution procedures have been established) function as preventive measures against more destructive outcomes. Grievance systems, for example, permit the step-by-step adjudication of differences to avoid major clashes between parties such as labor and management. Similarly, systems which provide for participation by the members of an organization in decision making, while they are positively associated with the number of disputes between parties, are negatively associated with the number of major incidents between them (Corwin, 1969). Thus, it might be accurate to say that intimacy between parties tends to result in disagreements which, in turn, reduce the likelihood of major fights and disruption.

The stimulation of a search for new facts or solutions

As pointed out earlier, at least some aspects of our social systems are automatic and predictable. Where social systems are functioning mechanically, however, there is little likelihood of creativity or change. On the other hand, when parties are involved in a disagreement the process may lead to a clarification of facts, thus facilitating the resolution of conflict. For example, if a wife tells her husband, "You are not doing your share of the housework," and the husband replies, "Yes, I am," then little may be resolved. However, if the husband replies, "What statements or behavior of mine have led to your conclusion that I am not assuming enough responsibility at home?" then the interaction is changed from a conflict to a problem-solving situation based on clarification of facts.

In another way, conflict can stimulate the search for new methods or solutions. When parties are in conflict about which of two alternatives to accept, their disagreement may stimulate a search for another solution mutually acceptable to both. In like manner, when both parties view themselves as seeking to gain an adequate share of scarce resources, they may actually find that their needs or goals can be met simultaneously with the development of creative solutions which neither had previously considered.

As these situations suggest, conflict can create tension which is reduced through problem solving. The tension acts as a stimulus to find new methods for its own reduction. This is the difference between *confrontation* and the way in which confrontation is resolved. The confrontations between labor and management, between students and college administrators, or between blacks and whites act as stimuli for change, stimuli which may lead to disruption or overt hostility or which may lead to new relationships between the parties and creative solutions to problems.

An increase in group cohesion and performance

Conflictive situations between two or more groups are likely to increase both the cohesiveness and the performance of the groups, although we must be careful to distinguish between effects during the conflict and those after the winner and loser have been identified. During the conflict members of each group close ranks and are united in their efforts. Members' evaluations of their own group improve (Blake and Mouton, 1961c); and each group judges its own solution as best. The positions of opponents are evaluated negatively, and there is little effort to understand them. Questions asked opponents are designed to embarrass or to weaken them rather than to generate facts and understanding. Perceptions of the group's own position are distorted, as is recognition of areas of common agreement with the opposing group. Even when the adversary's position is thought to be well understood by members of one group, research has shown that a real understanding is blocked by identification with the position of one's own group. In these circumstances intergroup resolution of conflict increases in difficulty since groups are most likely unaware of the distortions in factual knowledge that exist between them (Blake and Mouton, 1961a).

During the competitive period, levels of work and cooperation within each group are high. When competing groups select representatives to deal with other groups, they choose task leaders (hard-driving individuals who keep their own group on course) rather than individuals skilled in social facilitation. During conflict such leaders exhibit high loyalty to their group and tend to conform to group expectations rather than to focus upon the assigned problem (Blake and Mouton, 1961b).

Such conditions appear to be desirable, for the most part, and probably account for the popular belief that competition is valuable as a stimulus to work groups. But what actually happens when one group is declared the victor and the other the vanquished? For one thing, the leader of the winning group increases in status, while the leader of the losing group decreases in status. The leader in the losing group is blamed for the loss. The atmosphere in the groups also changes. The rate of tension, problem avoidance, fighting, and competitive feelings will increase in the losing group and decrease in the winning group. If the loss can be blamed on conditions beyond the control of the group, the result may be increased cohesion in the losing group (Lott and Lott, 1965). If the group does assume responsibility for the loss, it often analyzes the situation and prepares itself to fight better the next time. In contrast, the winning group merely says, "We did a good job. Let's knock off" (Blake and Mouton, 1961c, p. 432). Thus, heightened cooperation and effort by group members during the conflict may actually decrease once the conflict is resolved.

The measure of power or ability

Conflict provides a readily available method of measurement. If the ground rules for victory or defeat are identifiable to both parties, then the winner of a game or sports event can be easily determined. Such literal interpretation has cognitive value. In addition, while not precisely measurable, the relative power between parties may be identified through conflictive situations. Coercion, control, and suppression require clear superiority of power of one party over another, whereas problem solving requires an equalization of power among the parties. Thus, a party wishing to avoid overt suppression of the opponent must take action to provide a favorable power balance; suppression of the opponent can be avoided by employing problem-solving methods which insure a balance of power.

From the preceding discussion it should be clear that conflict is a process which itself is neither good nor bad, but which has elements and outcomes which may be judged favorably or unfavorably by those participating in or evaluating it. We shall now turn to the conflict process itself.

THE CONFLICT PROCESS

Conflict is defined in this book as a process which takes place between two or more parties.[1] By *parties* we may be referring to individ-

1. *This section draws from the work of Pondy (1967, 1969); Corwin (1969); Walton and Dutton (1969); Fink (1968); and Schmidt (1973).*

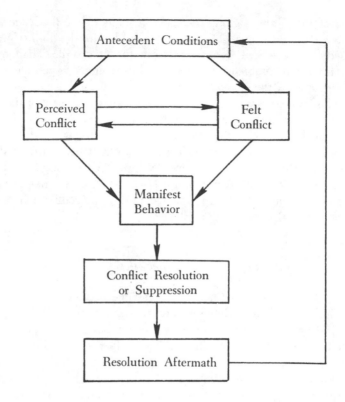

FIGURE 1–1.   The Conflict Process.

uals, groups, or organizations. The six steps in the process are depicted in Figure 1–1.

    1) Antecedent conditions are the characteristics of a situation which generally lead to conflict, although they may be present in the absence of conflict as well.

    2) Perceived conflict is a logically and impersonally recognized set of conditions which are conflictive to the parties.

    3) Felt conflict is a personalized conflict relationship, expressed in feelings of threat, hostility, fear, or mistrust.

    4) Manifest behavior is the resulting action—aggression, competition, debate, or problem solving.

    5) Conflict resolution or suppression has to do with bring-

ing the conflict to an end either through agreement among all parties or the defeat of one.

6) Resolution aftermath comprises the consequences of the conflict.

We shall now consider each part of the conflict process in more detail. An understanding of the factors that lead to conflict is necessary if its occurrence is to be minimized.

THE ANTECEDENT CONDITIONS OF CONFLICT

Listed below are nine characteristics of social relationships that are associated with various kinds or degrees of conflictive behavior.

1) *Ambiguous jurisdictions.* Conflict will be greater when the limits of each party's jurisdiction are ambiguous. When two parties have related responsibilities for which actual boundaries are unclear, the potential for conflict between them increases. Conversely, when role definitions are clear, each party can expect a certain type of behavior from the other, and fewer opportunities for disagreement occur. For example, the argument of a married couple about who should make decisions relating to household chores or the selection of evening entertainment was resolved by an agreement that on alternate days one of them would make all decisions and would be responsible for the success or failure of the decisions. On a more complex level, large organizations will define boundaries of individual responsibility through such tools as organization charts and job descriptions.

2) *Conflict of interest.* Conflict will be greater where a conflict of interest exists between the parties. One such situation is a competition for scarce resources. For example, one summer a married couple found themselves arguing about the use of the only air-conditioned room in their apartment, which also contained the television set. The woman was attending graduate school and the man was working; in the evening he wanted to watch baseball games on television and she wanted to use the room for study, complaining that the noise of the television prevented her from concentrating. Another

situation involves a case where the gain of one group is at the expense of another group. For example, Walton, Dutton, and Cafferty (1969) describe such an incident in which a maintenance department is evaluated on the basis of equipment performance. However, the equipment performance in a department served by maintenance is not part of the maintenance evaluation. The second department makes demands upon maintenance to increase its own performance record but in so doing reduces the rating of the maintenance department by interfering with the repair of other equipment.

3) *Communication barriers.* Conflict will be greater when barriers to communication exist. It appears that if parties are separated from each other physically or by time—for example, day shift versus night shift—the opportunity for conflict is increased. One explanation for this is the increased possibility of misunderstanding between the parties. Yet, as will be discussed shortly, the degree of knowledge which one party has about another is shown to be associated with conflict (Walton, Dutton, and Cafferty, 1969). It seems more likely that space or time separations create natural groupings which promote separate group interests rather than advance a common effort toward joint goals.

4) *Dependence of one party.* Conflict will be greater where one party is dependent upon another. Where one party must rely on another for performance of a task or for the provision of needed resources, the opportunity for conflict to occur is increased. A variety of situations probably contribute to such conflicts. For example, a leader may fail to define expected performance on the part of subordinates, leading to undesired outcomes and frustration. Or, expected coordination between two groups may not take place, leading to mutual accusation of faulty behavior.

5) *Differentiation in organization.* Conflict will be greater as the degree of differentiation in an organization increases. Where people work together in complex organizations, the: is evidence (Corwin, 1969) that measures of conflict are relate to the number of organizational levels, the number of distinc job specialties represented, and the degree to which labor divided in the organization. The reasons may well relate t conditions already discussed. For example, the number of leve of authority may create difficulties of communication, conflic

of interest, difficult dependency situations, or jurisdictional disputes. In any case, the greater the degree of differentiation, the greater the potential for conflict.

6) *Association of the parties.* Conflict will be greater as the degree of association of the parties increases. *Degree of association,* as used here, refers both to the parties' participation in decision making and to informal relations between them. Where parties make decisions jointly, the opportunity for conflict is greater, which may explain the reluctance of some managers to involve others in decision making. However, since groups often make superior decisions, the failure to utilize the potential of groups in decision making may be costly in terms of inferior judgments as well as in terms of employee dissatisfaction. An alternative logic would suggest that where participative decision making is used, the parties will need skills in conflict resolution. General conflict measures are positively associated with the degree of participation, although major incidents of conflict decrease as participation increases (Corwin, 1969).

The above holds true for informal association as well. Interaction and the degree of knowledge which parties have about each other are also related to rates of conflict.

7) *Need for consensus.* Conflict will be greater where consensus between the parties is necessary. When all parties must agree on a decision, at least to the point that no individual feels the decision is unacceptable, it is not surprising that disagreements will occur. Thus, it is possible to avoid conflict by having mechanisms such as voting, coin flipping, or adjudication to make decisions without the confrontation of consensus. As we shall see later, however, such mechanisms themselves are not without undesirable consequences.

8) *Behavior regulations.* Conflicts will be greater where behavior regulations are imposed. Regulating mechanisms include standardized procedures, rules, and policies. Regulating mechanisms seem to do two things at the same time. On the one hand, they reduce the likelihood of conflict since they serve to make relationships predictable and reduce the need to make arbitrary decisions. On the other hand, they increase the degree of control over parties, and this control may be resisted. If the adherence to or the imposition of rules becomes discretionary, further sources of disagreement are

created. Furthermore, if the parties have high individual needs for autonomy and self-control, it is likely that the presence of regulating procedures will lead to conflict.

9) *Unresolved prior conflicts.* Conflicts will be greater as the number of unresolved prior conflicts increases. As will be discussed later, the type of conflict resolution utilized will affect the resolution aftermath. Thus, prior experiences of the parties will themselves create antecedent conditions. Suppression of conflict by the use of power, or compromises to which the parties are uncommitted, create conditions and expectations which may lead to behavior conducive to further conflict.

The antecedent conditions need not lead directly to conflict, but they are certainly conditions which create opportunities for conflict to arise. Further development of overt conflict depends upon the perception of conditions which exist and the attitudinal characteristics of the parties.

PERCEIVED CONFLICT

Perceptions of the conditions which exist between the parties may enhance the likelihood of conflict or may reduce it. The failure to identify potentially conflictive conditions may prevent conflicts from developing. In many cases, however, it is the inaccurate or illogical perception of the situation which leads to overt conflict between the parties. Perceptual processes contribute to conflict in two ways. First, they provide an accurate or inaccurate assessment of the conditions which exist. This occurs when, for example, clear jurisdictions are perceived as ambiguous or when similar interests are perceived as conflicting. Second, they affect the extent to which the parties see the situation as one threatening a potential loss. The latter occurs when each party fails to recognize the availability of solutions which will satisfy the needs or requirements of both parties.

In the case of the couple in conflict about the use of the air-conditioned room containing the television set, the perceptions of one air-conditioned room and one television set were accurate. In fact, overt conflict resulted from this perception of the situation, and the conditions of dissimilar interests and scarce resources led to fighting behavior, as would be expected. Yet the perception of the problem could be and, in fact, was changed to suggest that the common interest was to find a way so that the wife could study in a quiet air-conditioned room and the husband could hear and watch the ball game in the air-conditioned room. Solutions to the conflict could be interpreted as unlimited when one considers not just the actual materials involved but the available combinations of these materials. In this particular case, the changed perceptions led to overt problem-solving behavior rather than conflict. The husband watched the game on television with the sound off and listened to the game through earphones. The wife then studied with her back to the television set.

Conflicts may also be perceived when antecedent conditions do not exist (Pondy, 1967). Such situations occur when the parties do not understand each other's actual positions or when either of the positions taken is based upon a limited knowledge of the facts. Both cases lend themselves to resolution by discussion between the parties to clarify the facts. In such situations, the difficulty lies not so much in the perceptual process and its clarification as it does in the attitudinal issues which arise when the parties become angry, mistrustful, or defensive. If these negative attitudes can be controlled, the eventual resolution is facilitated by discussion and clarification.

For example, if two arts administrators are planning a summer concert for a community and both agree that the objective is maximum entertainment value for the greatest number of people in the community, then the selection between two alternatives can be made easily by obtaining facts about the appeal of each to various client groups and by choosing the alternatives with the most appeal. Or, when two fishermen state potentially conflictive preferences for fishing deep or fishing shallow, the logical process is one of asking why each prefers his strategy and of determining more facts, in hope of finding a goal compatible to both fishermen and to their mutual goal of catching fish.

Finally, initial perceptions of conflict may result in conflict-avoiding processes. Two important methods which lead to this outcome are the suppression mechanism and the attention-focus mechanism (Pondy, 1967). The former occurs when individuals ignore conflictive situations that involve low potential loss or are viewed as minimally threatening (Blake, Mouton, and Shepard, 1964). The attention-focus mechanism occurs because parties can selectively perceive conflictive conditions and make choices about those to which they wish to attend.

It is likely that individuals attend more readily to those conflictive conditions which are perceived to have readily accessible processes for resolution or for which readily accessible outcomes are available. There also seems to be a preference for attending to those conflictive situations involving relatively fewer negative attitudes. Thus, the parties in a labor-management disagreement may focus on issues which lend themselves to established grievance systems or arbitration procedures and effectively ignore fundamental differences which cannot be handled routinely in the usual way. They may also be reluctant to deal with issues provoking anger and hostility and instead restrict attention to matters which do not create such feelings.

From the above discussion it may be seen that perceptual processes can act to create conflict or to avoid existing conflictive situations. The third important ingredient in the development of overt conflict or problem-solving behavior consists of the feelings or attitudes of the parties.

FELT CONFLICT

Feelings and attitudes, like perceptions, may create conflict where rational elements would not suggest that it must arise; feelings and attitudes also play a part in avoiding conflict where it might be expected to occur. The most important consideration in determining the outcome of the conflict is whether the situation is personalized or depersonalized. Personalized situations are those in which the whole being of the other party is threatened or judged negatively. Depersonalized situations are those in which the behavior of the other party, or the characteristics of the relationship, are *described* as creating a problem, rather than judged as being responsible.

To illustrate, feelings or expressions of feelings which say "You are bad" are personalized; feelings or their expression which say "What you believe is different from what I believe" are depersonalized. Similarly, the statement "You threaten me" is personal, while "Your behavior leads to fear on my part" is depersonalized. Personalized situations create tension and anxiety; depersonalized situations lend themselves to problem solving. We shall see later how much the language that parties use with each other can affect the personalized or depersonalized nature of the situation.

Feelings and attitudes which set the stage for overt behavior also arise out of characteristics of the individual personality. There is not as much likelihood of overt conflict when parties who are yielding or anxious to please are dealing with parties who are dominant or self-seeking, as there is when the parties are both of the dominant type. A married couple in which one partner is dominant and the other is submissive will experience less overt conflict than one in which both are dominant or both are submissive.

The feelings and attitudes about the mutuality of the relationship will further affect eventual behavior. Where the parties value cooperation and believe that success in their relationship involves the attainment of the needs of both, the situation is less conflictive than when the parties value competition and believe that one can win only at the other's expense. Such attitudes not only affect their perceptions of the situation but also determine the way in which they will judge the availability of solutions. Again, mutuality of interests and scarcity of resources relate in part to the initial feelings and attitudes of the parties.

Finally, trust between the parties can strongly affect the outcome of a potentially conflictive situation. Trusting attitudes elicit recognition of the mutual vulnerability of the parties, which occurs in part through the sharing of information between them. Vulnerability is also exhibited through the sharing of control by the parties. In the absence of such trust, a party is more likely to withhold information in order to avoid the danger of having the other party use the information against him. If a party does give information, however, he is likely to distort it in order to maintain his own advantage. Similarly, each nontrusting party will try to maximize his control over the other and to minimize the control of the other over himself. Thus, the presence of trust may prevent potentially conflictive situations from arising, while its absence may create conflict where actual conditions do not seem to warrant it.

No attempt is made here to determine the origins of the attitudes and feelings held by the parties. Undoubtedly some are cultural, while others have their origin in developmental experiences, perceptual processes, or personal experiences. Whatever the source, these feelings become important determinants of the development and resolution of overt conflict between the parties.

MANIFEST BEHAVIOR

The actual overt behavior of the parties, based upon antecedent conditions, perceptions, and attitudes, may be exhibited as conflictive or problem solving. Where there is a conscious (though not necessarily deliberate) attempt by one party to block the goal achievement of another party, the behavior may be considered to be conflictive (Pondy, 1967). Thus, when one party accidentally blocks the goal attainment of another, it is a chance occurrence in a social system. But when one party knowingly interferes with another, conflict is said to occur.

On the other hand, when the parties make conscious attempts to achieve the goals of both by supportive efforts, the behavior is that of problem solving. As with conflict behavior, the accidental achievement of both sets of goals is a chance occurrence; the deliberate effort to achieve them is overt problem-solving behavior. Parenthetically, it may be noted that the methodology of conflict is learned early in life and is well practiced. Competition, dominance, aggression, and defense are part of an established process unconsciously learned in the family, in the school, and in other social institutions. Problem solving, on the other hand, appears to be learned less frequently through developmental experiences. Conscious effort is generally required to develop and practice problem-solving skills.

Manifest conflict-resolution or problem-solving behavior may be described according to the degree to which it is programmed or unprogrammed. Programmed behavior follows specified or anticipated patterns in order to achieve outcomes readily identifiable by the parties. Its effectiveness is determined by the breadth of alternative behaviors available for utilization by the parties. For example, the skill of a chess player depends upon his ability to choose appropriately from among a wide variety of strategic moves. Similarly, the simulation of war through war games is designed to increase the variety of strategies and tactics available to the participants and to anticipate action-reaction sequences. Thus, programmed behavior is rational behavior.

Unprogrammed behavior in conflict resolution or in problem solving does not follow known patterns and is governed more by emotion. The appearance of anger, aggression, apathy, or rigidity in conflictive situations reduces each party's effectiveness in gaining a relative advantage and makes it difficult for both to terminate the interaction. For that reason, it is useful to program the conditions surrounding the relationship when it is not possible to program the actual action-reaction sequences. For example, where the boundaries between the parties cannot be made unambiguous, it is more useful to provide mechanisms for resolving boundary issues than it is to leave such resolution to chance. Such is the case when two departments with overlapping responsibilities establish a coordinating committee to deal with unanticipated issues that could potentially lead to conflict between them.

In like manner, problem solving may be handled on an unprogrammed emotional basis or it may be handled rationally. Communal or cooperative groups, united by strong emotional ties, often attempt to use consensual methods in their interactions. While the problem resolutions may be acceptable, the lack of programming and the scarcity of consciously identified alternative behaviors make such processes lengthy and susceptible to failure (Filley, 1973).

Finally, manifest behavior may be identified as that of an individual or that of a group. In this book we shall not distinguish between the two as parties in overt conflict unless making specific references to one or the other. Behavior between groups rather than individuals does not alter the basic pattern in the conflict process itself.

CONFLICT RESOLUTION OR SUPPRESSION

The next step in the conflict process is that of conflict resolution or suppression. Although the activity here is directed at ending the manifest conflict, in many cases it may resemble a continuation of the manifest conflict or problem-solving activity. It is distinguishable from such manifest behavior by the processes of conflict reduction rather than conflict elevation. In competition, the resolution process is simple and programmed: Rules specify the outcome. In less programmed and more disruptive conflicts, resolution involves the imposition of a deliberate strategy of conflict reduction.

In the next chapter we shall identify a number of conflict resolution mechanisms. These involve three types or classes according to results: (1) a win for some parties and a loss for others; (2) a partial gain and a partial loss for all parties; and (3) an acceptable gain for all parties. We are chiefly concerned in this book with the third type, generally referred to as problem solving and identified specifically as (a) consensus and (b) integrative decision making (IDM).

RESOLUTION AFTERMATH

Usually the resolution of conflict leaves a legacy which will affect the future relations of the parties and their attitudes about each other. Perhaps the most neutral in its effects is the end of a simple competitive situation viewed impersonally as an event. In such cases the value of the competitive process probably outweighs the attitudes about the final victory or defeat. More often, however, the outcome of a conflict leaves the parties with positive or negative changes in resources and with attendant feelings which are also positive or negative.

As pointed out earlier in this chapter, a clear defeat may leave a party with antagonistic or self-destructive feelings that merely set the stage for further conflict. Losers intend to win on the next encounter and such determination necessarily is accompanied by less cooperation, less trust, more personalization of the role of both parties, and distorted communication between the parties.

Where the resolution is one of compromise, the agreement often involves some form of future reciprocity. The parties become bound together by some kind of antagonistic cooperation. Often both parties will judge that they have given more than they have received; and, although neither party loses all, they both may have feelings of defeat (Burke, 1970). Parties will prepare themselves for a better bargain in the next encounter and, as in the previous case, will exhibit less trust, more personalization, and more frequent distortions in communication. Perhaps most important, they will often tend to manifest a low level of commitment to the compromise agreement (Blake, Mouton, and Shepard, 1964).

Finally, where problem solving results in an integrative outcome which is viewed as a win by both sides, the parties are brought closer together. Cooperation increases, future issues are depersonalized, trust is enhanced, and communication is accurate and complete. Problem solving is likely to leave the parties with a high level of commitment to the agreement.

To summarize, we have outlined the sequence associated with the development and resolution of conflict. Antecedent conditions, plus perceptions and attitudes, generate manifest behavior of a conflictive or problem-solving nature which is followed by some mechanism for ending the overt behavior. The resolution may be one which increases the likelihood of future conflicts or one which contributes to future harmony and cooperation. In the next chapter we shall discuss various methods of conflict resolution and problem solving.

NOTE ON EXPERIENTIAL LEARNING

Exercise 2 in the Appendix, "Conditions That Lead to Conflict or Cooperation," may be used in any real organization to determine the presence of conditions antecedent to conflict.

REFERENCES

Blake, R. R., and J. S. Mouton. "Comprehension of own and outgroup positions under intergroup competition." *Journal of Conflict Resolution* 5 (1961a): 304–10.

Blake, R. R., and J. S. Mouton. "Loyalty of representatives to ingroup positions during intergroup competition." *Sociometry* 24 (1961b): 177–83.

Blake, R. R., and J. S. Mouton. "Reactions to intergroup competition under win-lose conditions." *Management Science* 7 (1961c): 420–35.

Blake, R. R., J. S. Mouton, and H. A. Shepard. *Managing Intergroup Conflict in Industry.* Gulf, 1964.

Boulding, K. B. "A pure theory of conflict applied to organizations." In *The Frontiers of Management Psychology,* G. Fish, ed., Harper & Row, 1964.

Burke, R. J. "Methods of resolving superior-subordinate conflict: The constructive use of subordinate differences and disagreements." *Organizational Behavior and Human Performance* 5 (1970): 393–411.

Corwin, R. G. "Patterns of organizational conflict." *Administrative Science Quarterly* 14 (1969): 507–21.

Filley, A. C. "Organization invention: A study of utopian organizations." Wisconsin Business Papers No. 3. Bureau of Business Research and Service, University of Wisconsin-Madison, 1973.

Fink, C. F. "Some conceptual difficulties in the theory of social conflict." *Journal of Conflict Resolution* 13 (1968): 413–58.

Lott, A., and B. E. Lott. "Group cohesiveness as interpersonal attraction: A review of relationships with antecedent and consequent variables." *Psychological Bulletin* 64 (1965): 259–309.

Pondy, L. R. "Organizational conflict: Concepts and models." *Administrative Science Quarterly* 12 (1967): 296–320.

Pondy, L. R. "Varieties of organizational conflict." *Administrative Science Quarterly* 14 (1969): 499–506.

Rapoport, A. *Fights, Games, and Debates.* University of Michigan, 1960.

Schmidt, S. M. "Lateral conflict within employment service district offices." Unpublished doctoral dissertation, University of Wisconsin-Madison, 1973.

Walton, R. E., and J. M. Dutton. "The management of interdepartmental conflict: A model and review." *Administrative Science Quarterly* 14 (1969): 73–84.

Walton, R. E., J. M. Dutton, and T. P. Cafferty. "Organizational context and interdepartmental conflict." *Administrative Science Quarterly* 14 (1969): 522–43.

Methods
of Conflict Resolution
and Problem Solving

2

In the first chapter we discussed how conflicts develop. We shall now turn our attention to the ways in which conflicts are resolved. By *conflict resolution* we mean the termination of manifest conflict between individuals or groups. In some cases, such as compromise, the termination may leave both sides only partially committed to the resulting agreement. In other cases, the termination may provide high commitment to the resulting agreement. The methods of conflict resolution which we shall label *problem-solving* are those which find ways to meet goals or overcome obstacles in a manner which provides high-quality decisions that are acceptable to the parties involved in or affected by the decisions. While problem solving can take place without prior conflict, our focus in this book is on turning conflicts into problem-solving situations.

STRATEGIES FOR DEALING WITH CONFLICT

In this chapter and throughout this book, we shall be discussing three basic strategies for dealing with conflict: the win-lose strategy, the lose-lose strategy, and the win-win strategy. Although the last has relative advantages, win-lose and lose-lose strategies are widely practiced, perhaps because of the tendency many of us have to persist in using learned behavior patterns, even those which are destructive. As is obvious from their labels, both the win-lose and the lose-lose strategies involve the failure of at least one party to achieve his objective; as we shall see later, the only thing lost through the win-win strategy is the creation of losers.

WIN-LOSE METHODS

The first win-lose method is exemplified by the typical exercise of authority. When a supervisor says, "You must do what I say because I am the boss," he is exercising legitimate power bestowed upon him by the organization. Such authority allows him to reward and punish organization members within his area of control. In a second and related method, mental or physical power is used to bring about the compliance of another individual or group, as in the case where a supervisor covertly or overtly threatens a subordinate with dismissal if he dares disagree. A third win-lose method involves a failure to respond. For example, if, in a company sales conference dealing with a problem of reduced sales in some territories, Sam says, "I think we ought to reorganize the territories among salesmen," and no one responds to Sam, his idea goes "plop." He loses and everyone else wins. Given several experiences of this sort, Sam may withdraw from further discussion, thereby avoiding the pain of losing.

A fourth win-lose method employs majority rule. The democratic ethic is centered around voting on issues. In addition, there is empirical evidence that the majority is more often correct than the minority. Yet, as this book will demonstrate, there are ways to achieve good decisions without creating a losing group through voting. Voting seems to be a suitable strategic operation when a group meets together over time; members sometimes vote on the winning side and sometimes on the losing side, and the alternatives voted upon are reasonably acceptable to all. However, when a minority continuously loses and when such losses are viewed as personal defeats, then majority rule can be quite destructive.

A fifth win-lose method employs minority rule. There are two common examples of this approach. The first example of minority rule is the chairman of a meeting saying, "I think we have enough work to warrant a meeting at the same time next week; what do you think?" If there is no response, the chairman then manipulates silence into support for his own position, saying, "Since no one disagrees, we'll have a meeting next week." We would not be surprised if the subsequent meeting were poorly attended. The second example of minority rule occurs when an issue is "railroaded" through a meeting by only a few supporters. That is, if three people in a group of nine agree to support a proposal prior to the meeting, the strength of their agreement may intimidate the majority at the actual meeting. For example, Mr A might say, "I propose that we do X." His supporters B and C then might vocalize their strong support of the issue. But Mr. D may say, "I haven't heard this proposal before, but there is something about it that bothers me and I'm not sure that I like it." Then A, B, and C may say to D, "Well, you're a little thickheaded" or "You don't seem to understand why this is a good method" or "You're obstructing progress." At this point, other group members, not wanting to be similarly embarrassed or put down, may remain silent; and without further dissent the minority position may emerge as the official position of the group.

LOSE-LOSE METHODS

These methods are so named because neither side really accomplishes what it wants or, alternately, each side only gets part of what it wants. Lose-lose methods are based on the assumptions that half a loaf is better than none, and avoidance of conflict is preferable to personal confrontation on an issue. A popular lose-lose method employs compromise. Curiously, if an individual says, "I will compromise my values," *compromise* has a clearly negative connotation. On the other hand, when two parties arrive at a settlement to a dispute and announce a compromise, the word may be viewed positively. As used in this book, the word has a negative connotation. While compromise is sometimes necessary, it is an unfortunate second best to win-win strategies.

A second lose-lose strategy involves side payments. In essence, one who offers a side payment means, "I will bribe you to take a losing position." Organizations use side payments extensively and at great cost, paying individuals extra income to do disagreeable tasks; thereby both sides are partial losers.

A third lose-lose strategy calls for submitting an issue to a neutral third party. Thus, when two department managers ask their common superior to decide on an issue about which they are in conflict, they avoid confrontation and problem solving in favor of a process which each hopes will yield at least some benefit to himself. Similarly, when two parties in a labor dispute submit the issue to arbitration, they do so in the hope that their individual positions will be enhanced to some degree. When a third party resolves a dispute totally in favor of one disputant, this method may be viewed as win-lose. Arbitrators, however, frequently resolve issues at some middle ground between the positions held by disputants. Although it is to the advantage of the arbitrator, as well as of some value to the disputants, to have both sides gain at least something from the conflict resolution, the outcomes are rarely satisfactory to both sides.

A fourth lose-lose strategy involves the practice of resorting to rules—either those established on an ad hoc basis to resolve the issue, or rules already in existence. If, for example, two parties in a dispute decide to flip a coin to resolve it, they are neither problem solving nor confronting the issue; they are merely turning the problem over to the laws of chance. Similarly, when an employee asks for a day off to attend a funeral and his supervisor utilizes a rule as the basis for rejecting the request, problem solving is not achieved. Like arbitration, some rule-based strategies lead to win-lose resolutions while others lead to lose-lose outcomes. Rules are simply a way to avoid confrontation.

It should be noted at this point that both win-lose and lose-lose methods are based on disagreements about means—my way versus your way, Alternative A versus Alternative B. For example, sales and production administrators in business often argue about whether additional funds should be given to the sales department to enhance marketing or to the production department to improve manufacturing techniques. Even the common dinner-table arguments about whether or not a child should eat spinach are of this sort. The end goals (in the first example, increased profitability, and in the second, the health and happiness of the child) are typically not kept in focus during such discussions. The parties argue about means for solving the problem as each views it, rather than agreeing upon a common definition of an ultimate objective.

COMMON CHARACTERISTICS OF WIN-LOSE AND LOSE-LOSE METHODS

In summary, the methods discussed so far have several things in common:

1) There is a clear we-they distinction between the parties, rather than a we-versus-the-problem orientation.

2) Energies are directed toward the other party in an atmosphere of total victory or total defeat.

3) Each party sees the issue only from its own point of view, rather than defining the problem in terms of mutual needs.

4) The emphasis in the process is upon attainment of a solution, rather than upon a definition of goals, values, or motives to be attained with the solution.

5) Conflicts are personalized rather than depersonalized via an objective focus on facts and issues.

6) There is no differentiation of conflict-resolving activities from other group processes, nor is there a planned sequence of those activities.

7) The parties are conflict-oriented, emphasizing the immediate disagreement, rather than relationship-oriented, emphasizing the long-term effect of their differences and how they are resolved.

WIN-WIN METHODS

In contrast to the win-lose and lose-lose strategies discussed previously, win-win problem-solving strategies focus initially on ends or goals rather than on obvious and sometimes unnecessary alternatives. These strategies take two basic forms: consensus and integrative decision-making (IDM) methods.

Consensus decisions occur when, in a judgmental situation, a final solution is reached which is not unacceptable to anyone. Unlike other win-win methods, in a consensus decision there is no polarized conflict among parties involved and little arguing about means and ends of solving the problem at hand. For example, a popular simulation exercise asks groups of people to rank order a group of items in terms of their desirability for a trip across the moon. Hall (1971) has shown that when certain group-process rules are used, the group decision is frequently better than the best individual judgment. Similar results may be demonstrated in exercises which elicit people's responses to questions about the accurate interpretation of a simple story.

Typical process rules in such cases (Hall, 1972; Guetzkow and Gyr, 1954) suggest that participants: (1) focus upon defeating the problem rather than each other; (2) avoid voting, trading, or averaging; (3) seek facts to resolve dilemmas; (4) accept conflict as helpful, providing it does not elicit threats or defensiveness; (5) avoid self-oriented behavior when it portends the exclusion of others' needs or positions.

IDM methods differ more in degree than in kind from consensus strategies. Where consensus is used to solve judgmental problems of selecting from a variety of solution strategies, integrative methods are more concerned with sequencing the decision process through a series of steps. Integrative methods are particularly useful when the parties are polarized around a few solution strategies and need to work out a conflict situation. The particular emphasis in integrative methods is upon pooling the goals or values of parties after they have polarized.

As we have seen, most conflicts involve disagreements of means rather than ends—"*my* way" versus "*your* way." Such conflicts assume the existence of a fixed and frequently incompatible set of possible solutions, causing each party to argue about the superiority of its personal solution rather than joining with the opposing party to find a new solution which is acceptable to both. Perhaps for this reason, the experimental literature and simulations of conflict often deal with situations in which the gain of one party is equal to the loss of the other party. These are situations, for example, in which a fixed sum of money is to be divided between two parties and what one side gains the other must necessarily lose. These are known as "zero-sum" situations.

As we shall demonstrate, however, many situations which are thought to be zero-sum may be changed into a positive gain for *both* parties. To accomplish this, the parties must shift attention from solutions per se to the goals or motives of each and then seek solutions which permit both sides to obtain their needs. If the parties assume that the gain of one is the loss of the other, the process of resolution is one in which the parties use their energies against each other. If the parties employ problem-solving methods, they use their energies to defeat the problem.

Problem-solving strategies (consensus and IDM) require each party to express his needs. Such strategies create a climate in which each individual participates responsibly in the group, working to satisfy both his own needs and the needs of the other group members. Problem-solving strategies are not self-imposing. The reader may have noted from his own experience that those who seek to help others frequently do more damage than good. When an individual tries to do something nice for someone, gives a present to someone, or provides help to someone, he may be dictating what the other party *should* want rather than providing what the other party *does* want.

A person using problem-solving methods is saying three things to other parties involved:

1) *"I want a solution which achieves your goals and my goals and is acceptable to both of us."* As Figure 2–1 indicates, there are three levels of acceptance or lack of acceptance for ranking all possible solutions to a problem: Some alternatives will be supported by each member; some alternatives will not be unacceptable to each member; and some will be personally opposed by each member. Strategies of total agreement are confined to the first category; that is, they seek solutions which are supported by all of the members. In problem solving, on the other hand, the parties seek to find a solution which is not unacceptable to anyone—that is, which falls in either the "don't care" or the support category.

The rationale for this approach can be found in Norman Maier's (1963) suggestion that an effective decision is a product of *quality* times *acceptance*. Decision quality is based upon objective facts which indicate that one solution is superior to an alternative solution; for example, Solution A will yield more profit than Solution B. Decision acceptance is based upon the feelings of those involved in or affected by the decision; for example, Party A is willing to support and implement Solution X but is not willing to support and implement Solution Y. Quality and acceptance interact to the extent that a high quality solution which has no support may be less desirable than a solution of less quality which is acceptable to all the parties. The extent to which quality and acceptance are factors in a decision will, of course, vary from situation to situation.

Problems may be analyzed and proper solution methods determined by focusing on quality and acceptance factors. Thus, we have the following four categories:

a) *High concern for quality, low concern for acceptance.*

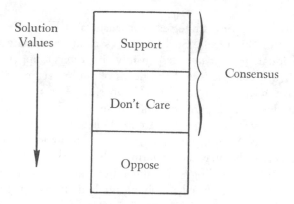

FIGURE 2–1.   Solution Values and Consensus.

Such decisions do not entail emotional considerations on the part of the people who must implement them. For example, product-pricing decisions, order quantity decisions, or acquisition decisions will not be successful or unsuccessful according to whether or not people support the decisions. Where time is an important consideration, such decisions will probably be made by individuals. Where solution quality is important and the decisions do not involve routine calculations, they might best be made by small problem-solving groups (Filley and House, 1969, Chapter 7).

b) *High concern for acceptance, low concern for quality.* Some decisions have a variety of solutions which differ little from each other in terms of quality. The issue involved in these decisions is simply one of fairness and equity. For example, if a manager has five foremen and one football ticket that he wishes to give to one of them, equity rather than quality is the primary consideration. Under such conditions, the manager would be well advised to turn the problem over to the foremen for their group decision.

c) *High concern for quality, high concern for acceptance.* Some decisions involve both important quality considerations when evaluating alternatives and important emotional considerations which can alter the success of the solution. For example, when considering two production methods it may be determined that Method A should produce twenty-five units an hour while Method B should produce twenty units an hour. However, subjective considerations may determine the actual outcome if the method depends on the willingness of the employees to make it work. If Method A is clearly opposed by the workers, then the expected twenty-five units may not be realized; and, if Method B has the workers' support, it may be better to employ Method B. Decisions in this category are best made by small groups composed of representatives who are sources of factual quality information and representatives who can accurately assess acceptance.

d) *Low concern for quality, low concern for acceptance.* Some decisions involve little difference between alternatives in terms of quality and also involve alternatives which are equally acceptable. For example, a couple may have to make a decision concerning which of two movies to see. Such decisions are best handled by flipping a coin or some similar arbitrary method.

Thus, it will be seen that quality and acceptance will vary from decision to decision and that the decision strategy that is best will depend upon the balance of these factors.

2) *"It is our collective responsibility to be open and honest about facts, opinions, and feelings."* Where a proper group climate is established and members learn skills of group interaction, each one can focus upon his own needs and upon group goals. A member need not and probably should not try to express needs and feelings for other group members but may ask other group members to report their own feelings and objectives. For example, consider a group of three workers participating in the design of a work system having to do with three steps in a subassembly operation. The steps permit workers either to rotate between two positions, or to be assigned a permanent position at one of the three steps. If two workers see job rotation as a vehicle for their own satisfaction but one does not, rotation-minded individuals do not help the third worker by telling him that he *should* want to rotate. They may, however, ask the third worker to express the reasons behind his preference. If the third worker has a preference which he does not disclose, he has failed to take responsibility for his own needs in the decision process; and the other workers cannot be blamed for a final solution which does not satisfy those unspoken needs. Admittedly,

there are many forces in the development of an individual which teach him never to express his true feelings. We shall discuss this problem later, also suggesting how new attitudes may be developed.

3) *"I will control the process by which we arrive at agreement but will not dictate content."* Successful utilization of IDM requires that people follow certain prescribed rules for group process. IDM does not, however, prescribe what individual preferences or goals should be. The person controlling the process, if not a member of the conflict-resolution or problem-solving situation, needs only to make sure that the process is followed correctly. But if this person *is* part of the conflict-resolution or problem-solving situation, he has a perfect right to indicate what his own goals or preferences are—in effect saying, "I would like to find a solution in which you get what you want and I get what I want—that is, neither your solution nor my solution but a strategy which satisfies both of us."

Before the IDM process is described in detail, there are two points which should be made; they will be repeated for emphasis in later chapters. The first is that IDM does not ask, *"Can* we accomplish this goal or objective?"* for to ask that is to run the risk of preventing any problem solving. Instead, it asks, *"How* can we accomplish this goal or objective?"* and thus it fosters open and continual effort toward the objective of conflict resolution.

The second point is that the first element of conflict, the we-they distinction, frequently leads to a win-lose or a lose-lose resolution; and, as stated earlier, to create losers is costly. The process focus of IDM is on defeating the problem rather than defeating other people.

CURRENT RESEARCH ON CONFLICT RESOLUTION

Research on organizational behavior, on problem solving, and on bargaining behavior provides a basis for inferring the relative effects of the conflict-resolution methods described above. Lawrence and Lorsch (1967) examined the use of confrontation (win-win type methods), forcing (resorting to authority or coercion), and smoothing (agreeing on an intellectual or nonthreatening level) in six organizations. They concluded that the two highest performing organizations used confrontation to a greater degree than the other four organizations, and that the next two organizations, in order of performance, used confrontation more than the lowest two.

Burke (1970) has reported several studies comparing methods, the first of which asked seventy-four managers to describe the way they and their immediate superiors dealt with conflicts among them. Five different methods of resolution were identified—withdrawal, smoothing, compromise, forcing, and confrontation—and then each was related to dependent variables of constructive use of conflict and each method's relationship to planning and to evaluating job performance. Comparing results relating to the variable of constructive use of conflict, the more effective supervisors used the methods in the following order: 1) confrontation, 2) smoothing, 3) compromise, 4) forcing, and 5) withdrawal. The least effective supervisors used instead: 1) confrontation, 2) forcing, 3) withdrawal, 4) smoothing, and 5) compromise. While it is surprising that confrontation is reported most frequently in the less effective group as well as in the more effective group, the frequent use of forcing is not.

The ways in which various methods of conflict resolution are related to a measure of constructive use of conflict may be seen in Table 2-1. As indicated, the higher respondents rated on constructive use of conflict, the less they used forcing and withdrawal and the more they used confrontation and smoothing. Possibly, individuals use force

TABLE 2-1.   Pearson Correlation of Methods of Conflict Resolution with Constructive Use of Conflict. From "Methods of Resolving Superior-Subordinate Conflict: The Constructive Use of Subordinate Differences and Disagreements" by Ronald J. Burke. From *Organizational Behavior and Human Performance*, Vol. 5, No. 4, 1970, p. 400.

1) Withdrawal	$-.19^{**}$
2) Smoothing	$.20^{**}$
3) Compromise	$-.08$
4) Forcing	$-.26^{*}$
5) Confrontation	$.26^{*}$

N = 74 for all correlations.
 * Correlation is significantly different from zero at the .05 level of confidence
** Correlation is significantly different from zero at the .10 level of confidence

or confrontation when they see the stakes as high and withdrawal or smoothing when they see the stakes as low. Table 2–1 also shows that the use of compromise is unrelated, positively or negatively, to the constructive use of conflict.

When compared to measures such as reliance on planning, superior helpfulness, and joint goal setting, withdrawal was negatively related, smoothing and compromise were unrelated, forcing was negatively related, and confrontation was positively related to six of the seven dependent variables concerned with planning and evaluating job performance.

In a second study, Burke compared 53 descriptions of effective conflict resolution with 53 descriptions of ineffective conflict resolution obtained from 57 respondents. Of these, 58.5 percent of the effective statements were classed as confrontation, and 79.2 percent of the ineffective statements were classed as forcing. In general, the evidence strongly supports the greater effectiveness of win-win methods as compared with win-lose methods.

Another body of literature which sheds some light on the relative advantages of win-win methods has to do with simulations of bargaining behavior in groups of two. These bargaining simulations generally involve a buyer and a seller, with price and profit fixed in a payoff table. Unlike consensus and problem-solving studies, these studies focus on achieving an optimum contract instead of a judgment or ideal ranking. In addition, there is no qualitative shift in the process to a concern with motives or goals. Bargaining studies are useful in showing the relative effects of negotiation versus problem solving and in associating personality correlates with different types of bargainers.

For example, Lewis and Pruitt (1971) simulated negotiation between ninety-two undergraduates in which participants took either a one-sided orientation or a problem-solving orientation. Under the former condition, a negotiator was concerned only with his own needs; under the latter he was concerned with the other's position as well. Bargainers took a high or low aspiration to the payoffs, and they dealt with each other under one of two conditions: (1) a "free communication" condition, in which they could say anything; or (2) a "truthful communication" condition, in which they were constrained to tell the truth about payoffs. The total payoff of both parties proved to be higher under the problem-solving than under the one-sided condition, and greater under a high-aspiration than under a low-aspiration condition. The relationship between the two more successful conditions suggested that "when coupled with a problem-solving orientation, high aspirations encourage integrative bargaining and thereby enhance the chances of observing new alternatives that bring high joint payoff" (Lewis and Pruitt, 1971, p. 222). Thus, it would appear that win-win decision strategies (where the total payoff, not the individual payoff, is the measure of success) are associated with better judgments, more favorable organization experience, and more favorable bargains.

To further demonstrate the superiority of win-win decision strategies, consider the following account of a meeting held to discuss possible prison reforms in Wisconsin. Nine of the state's top prison officials met to design an ideal correctional institution. In the course of the discussion, one group member proposed that uniforms traditionally worn by prison guards be eliminated. The group then began a lengthy argument about whether or not uniforms should be worn. One group member suggested that the issue be resolved democratically by vote. As a result, six people voted against uniforms and three voted in favor of them. The winning members looked pleased while the losing members either got angry or withdrew from further discussion.

A group consultant present at the time suggested that the members take another look at the situation. Then he asked those in favor of uniforms what they hoped to accomplish. Those officials stated that part of the rehabilitative process in correctional institutions is that of teaching people to deal constructively with authority, and saw uniforms as a means for achieving that goal. When asked why they opposed uniforms, the other group members said that uniforms created such a stigma that guards had an additional difficulty laying to rest the stereotypes held by inmates before they could deal with them on a one-to-one basis. The group consultant then asked the group what ways might be appropriate to meet the combined goals, namely, teaching people to deal with authority and avoiding the difficulty of stereotypes held about traditional uniforms. While working on the problem, the group generated ten possible solutions, including identification of prison personnel by name tags, by color-coded casual dress, or by uniforms for guard supervisors but not for guards in constant contact with prisoners. After discussing the various alternatives, the group decided upon the third solution.

In their first discussion, the group engaged in clear-cut conflict which was only partially resolved by vote. In the discussion led by the consultant, the group turned to problem solving, eventually developing a win-win method which was acceptable to all parties concerned.

NOTE ON EXPERIENTIAL LEARNING

Exercise 1 in the Appendix, "Group Decision Making," will demonstrate the concept of consensus decision making and will also indicate the extent to which the consensus decision is likely to be better than the best individual decision in the group. Exercise participants should also notice the win-lose or lose-lose behaviors exhibited by group members.

REFERENCES

Burke, R. J. "Methods of resolving superior-subordinate conflict: The constructive use of subordinate differences and disagreements." *Organizational Behavior and Human Performance* 5 (1970): 393–411.

Filley, A. C., and R. J. House. *Managerial Process and Organizational Behavior*. Scott, Foresman, 1969.

Guetzkow, H., and J. Gyr. "An analysis of conflict in decision-making groups." *Human Relations* 7 (1954): 367–81.

Hall, J. "Decisions, decisions, decisions." *Psychology Today* 5 (1971): 51–58.

Hall, R. M. *Organizations: Structure and Process*. Prentice-Hall, 1972.

Lawrence, P. R., and J. W. Lorsch. *Organization and Environment: Managing Differentiation and Integration*. Division of Research, Graduate School of Business Administration, Harvard University, 1967.

Lewis, S. A., and D. G. Pruitt. "Organization, aspiration level, and communication freedom in integrative bargaining." *Proceedings of the American Psychological Association* 6 (1971): 221–22.

Maier, N. R. *Problem-Solving Discussions and Conferences: Leadership Methods and Skills*. McGraw-Hill, 1963.

The Language
of Conflict
and Problem Solving

3

This chapter describes the different uses of language in conflict and problem solving and suggests that the way we say something elicits a particular kind of response from a listener. As we shall see, the language of conflict is filled with personal threats, judgments, and defensiveness. The language of problem solving, on the other hand, is nonthreatening, descriptive, and factual.

TRANSACTIONAL ANALYSIS

One method for describing the language of problem solving has been developed by Eric Berne and Thomas Harris in a number of books (Berne, 1961; Harris, 1969). They call their method of describing interpersonal and intrapersonal processes transactional analysis. When one party says something to another, and the second party responds in some way, a transaction has taken place.

Transactions are classified into three types, labeled *the Parent,* *the Adult,* and *the Child.* It will be helpful to the reader to think of these labels as arbitrary designations, for they might have been conveniently labeled *Type 1, Type 2,* and *Type 3* transactions.

One way to understand the types is to think of a child being born with two tape recorders going at the same time. The first recorder, identified as *Parent,* tapes messages coming from outside of the child (largely from his parents). Such inputs are taken in at a time when it is impossible for the child to modify, correct, or explain them. One portion of these inputs is of a "how to" variety—how to eat, how to dress, and how to behave acceptably; another portion is composed of judgments and values—what one should do, what one should not do, what is good, and what is bad. Other sources of Parent data are television, other adults, and, once the child begins school, teachers.

The Child, on the other hand, is a recording of events within the individual. Child recordings are largely of feelings and fantasies. Since the child has relatively little vocabulary during his early years, these feelings may not have words and, in any case, are difficult to express. When a person is in the grip of feelings such as rage, sadness, or fear, it is said that his "Child" has taken over.

The child receives rewards and good experiences from the adult in the form of caressing, kindness, and reassurance, called *stroking* in the Harris-Berne jargon. But stroking is not sufficient to overcome a feeling on the part of the child that he is "not OK." Given only his Parent and Child recordings, the child concludes that others are "OK" while he is "not OK," for he is dependent, helpless, limited in his mobility, narrow in his range of interests, and subordinate, while the adult is independent, mobile, has a wide variety of interests, and is superior. In the context of our discussion, the child feels that he is losing while others, the adults, are winning. They know what is right and wrong; they teach him; they judge him; they control his behavior.

The individual who grows up with only a developed Parent and Child behavior characteristically engages in either "mountain climbing" or in looking for a superparent. That is, in the former he says to himself, "I'm not OK; but if I can only get that job or that promotion or that house, then I will be OK." Having attained his objective, he discovers that he still feels inadequate and decides that another job, another promotion, or another house must be the answer. In this sense, the "mountain climber" keeps looking for the magic solution to his problems. The individual looking for superparent does so for much the same reason. He says to himself, "I don't feel OK, but if I can just find the right superparent he can lay hands on me and say, 'You are OK.'" Such an individual seeks heroes, another magic solution, or, in the words of Harris, he "looks for big strokes from big folks."

From the standpoint of conflict and problem solving, it may be noted that judgments such as good/bad, right/wrong, should/should not will frequently elicit either Parent or Child responses from others, and obstruct the Adult-Adult interactions which are the basis of problem solving. When one person tells another that he is bad, the second is likely to do one of two things: (1) argue back or (2) exhibit anger or hurt if his Child behavior takes over. Moreover, the wishing and fantasy of Child behavior are not likely to help in constructive problem solving. The executive who says, "I wish we had more capital for expansion," may be simply avoiding the question "How can we achieve desired expansion in our business?"

The third category of transactions involves what Berne and Harris call Adult statements. While the Parent and the Child develop unconsciously or without much control by the individual, the Adult is developed deliberately through the acquisition of skills and understanding and a willingness to confront reality through taking personal responsibility. In this vein, the author has heard psychologist Carl Rogers describing a client saying, "I can't expect someone to give me an education. I'll really have to do it myself." Similarly, people who have experienced sensitivity training frequently say, "I have been letting other people define me and I have been carried along in my life by unplanned events. I'm ready to define myself and to determine my own life." Adult statements are descriptive rather than judgmental and involve giving and getting information. Thus, when an individual says, "You are frightening," he is making a Parent statement and a judgment. When he says, "I feel frightened when you engage in that behavior," he is making an Adult statement about his feelings. When an individual says, "You are wrong," he is making a Parent statement. When the second person responds, "Why do you think I am wrong?" he is responding with an Adult statement. Words like *why, what, where, who, when,* and *how* are Adult statements eliciting information. People may use their Adult behavior to check out their Parent recordings and establish Parent dimensions that are based on reality. For example, the white man may find that his stereotype of the black man is quite erroneous, eliminating that part of his Parent. On the other hand, another individual may establish a Parent rule that if it is January in Wisconsin, a person living there should wear a heavy coat.

The Adult may also discover the role of feelings and their effect on behavior. He may find that feelings are not good or bad, but that the use of feelings or response to feelings may have effects which help or hinder problem solving. For example, individuals who are overcome by emotion cannot use their Adult behavior effectively.

When each party in an interaction understands the role of the other, then interaction may proceed. Figure 3–1 depicts situations where stimulus statements and response statements are parallel. Conflicts generally contain Parent-to-Parent statements, that is, "I am right and you are wrong." Problem solving is characteristic of Adult-to-Adult statements, that is, "How can we find a solution which will satisfy our collective requirements?" Fun and games usually signify Child-to-Child interactions in the form of mutual stroking. Other combinations permit interaction as well, as long as both parties know what to expect from each other.

When expected roles differ, interaction is blocked. For example, when a wife says to her husband, "Did you buy a loaf of bread on the way home from work?" and the husband responds, "Why are you always nagging me?" their interaction is not complementary and will probably stop, unless it is possible to change the type of interaction. If a manager tells his secretary that she is doing a poor job, her natural response may be to cry as a child or to argue as a parent. If, instead, she says, "What is it that you don't like about my behavior?" she is asking an Adult question and may evoke a descriptive Adult response from the manager.

It should be noted that each of us has Parent, Adult, and Child behaviors. The Parent and Child develop without much thought; the Adult, however, requires conscious effort for its development. Our Parent contains rules of behavior and values which simplify our deal-

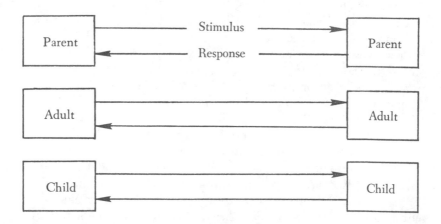

FIGURE 3–1.   Complementary Transactions. From *Transactional Analysis in Psychotherapy* by Eric Berne. Reprinted by permission of Grove Press, Inc. Copyright © 1961 by Eric Berne.

ings with a complex world but which should be checked out in reality. Our Child contains feelings and creativity which, if properly handled, may add to our personal joy and attractiveness to others. Our Adult contains the language of problem solving.

FEEDBACK AND SELF-DISCLOSURE

The language of conflict often elicits feelings of threat or defensiveness; that is, it closes people off from each other. On the other hand, the language of problem solving elicits trust and positive regard for openness. Put another way, to the extent that we share information in common, including details about each other's knowledge, attitudes, and behavior, without feelings of threat or defensiveness, we have a broader range of problem-solving potential.

This notion is illustrated in the Johari Window in Figure 3–2. The Johari Window depicts the relationship between two parties, you and me. There are certain things that you know about yourself and others that you don't know. There are certain things that I know

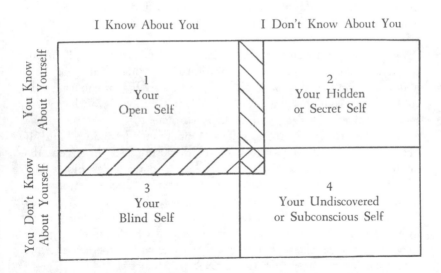

FIGURE 3–2.   Johari Window. Reprinted from *Of Human Interaction* by Joseph Luft by permission of National Press Books. Copyright © 1969 by the National Press.

about you and others that I don't know about you. As indicated, these perspectives may be combined to describe four positions for you.

Cell 1 is your open self in which what I know about you corresponds with what you know about yourself. This is the area in which we communicate most effectively. Our words, thoughts, and ideas mean the same thing. There is no need for feelings of threat or defensiveness.

Cell 2 in the Johari Window is your secret self, containing those things that I do not know about you but that you know about yourself. The secret self may occur because you do not trust me and do not want to make yourself vulnerable to me. In effect, you may be saying, "There are certain things which I am afraid to reveal about myself—my fears, my failures, my weaknesses—because I am not sure whether you will hurt or exploit me with that information."

The third cell in the model is your blind self, containing those things that I know about you but you do not know about yourself. For example, you may have certain mannerisms which you do not know about or you may speak in a way which makes it difficult for me to understand you. I can reduce your blind self by giving you such information, yet I may be reluctant to do so for fear of hurting your feelings or making you angry. As will be indicated shortly, there are some guidelines which will make it easier to reduce the blind self without negative consequence.

The fourth cell in the Johari Window is your undiscovered or subconscious self, containing information which I do not know about you and you do not know about yourself. If you can gain some information about this undiscovered self, it may make you happier or more effective in dealing with your environment.

The secret self in the Johari Window may be reduced and the open self increased by processes of self-disclosure. To the extent that an individual increases his trust in others and decreases his feelings of threat or defensiveness, he may feel freer to disclose information about himself. In addition, by practicing self-disclosure an individual is able to test reality. As Victor Frankl points out, it is common for individuals to experience more anxiety about what might happen if they disclose facts about themselves than is actually experienced when such facts are revealed (Frankl, 1963).

The blind self is reduced and the open self increased by processes of feedback. While it is not uncommon for people to refrain from giving feedback for fear of hurting the recipient or making him angry, proper feedback procedures will minimize such responses on the part of the recipient. When both the secret and the blind selves are reduced, an individual may discover information which was previously unknown. This experience may release a creative self as well.

RULES FOR FEEDBACK

Problem solving is facilitated when all parties have the same information. Thus, preparation for problem solving requires the establishment of an open relationship between parties. Just as an individual can learn to deal at the Adult level of transactional analysis rather than at the Parent and Child levels, so an individual can learn to give feedback in a manner which minimizes judgment, fear, threat, and defensiveness. The following seven rules are helpful in this regard (National Training Laboratories, 1968):

1) *Be descriptive rather than judgmental.* For example, when a supervisor tells an employee that the employee is getting lazy, the employee's response is more likely to be pained or angry than if the supervisor says, "Your average productivity this month is 20 percent below your average for the last six months." As indicated earlier in this chapter, judgmental statements, described as Parent transactions, tend to trigger Parent or Child responses in the recipient. On the other hand, descriptive statements are Adult transactions and provide raw material for problem solving.

2) *Be specific rather than general.* Feedback is more effective when it describes specific behavior and incidents. If I say to a person, "The way you talk to me makes me angry," I give him far less help than if I say, "When I tried to talk to you just now, you interrupted me and seemed not to be interested in what I was saying." Similarly, for an employee to tell his boss that they have a problem of communication is less effective than for the employee to say, "I have just discovered that you gave an order to my subordinate this morning and did not inform me." Since the details are more likely to be fresh in the minds of the people involved, it should also be clear that effective feedback is facilitated when examples of specific instances of recent behavior are utilized rather than references to past general patterns of behavior.

3) *Deal with things that can be changed.* Feedback is most effectively used when it concerns behavior which the recipient can

change. For example, an individual has little control over his height; however, he can control how he phrases his questions, how he dresses, or where he sits at a meeting. The purpose of feedback is to help the recipient, and it therefore must focus on things that the recipient can change or control. There may be cases, however, in which feedback dealing with uncontrollable factors is also useful. If a manager has a different racial background than an employee, it may help the employee to know that the manager has a stereotype concerning the employee's race which affects the manager's reaction to that individual.

4) *Give feedback when it is desired.* The processes which we are describing require effort and understanding on the part of both the giver and the receiver of feedback; for this reason it is a good idea to check with the recipient to find out whether he actually wants such information. If for some reason he is already feeling defensive or depressed, he will not be helped by the disclosure, and feedback should be appropriately reserved until some later time.

5) *Consider the motives for giving and receiving feedback.* It is a good idea to check why one really wants to give such information to another. Where the giver is in effect saying, "I'm doing this for your own good," he frequently means, "It gives me pleasure to be able to tell you these things." Self-gratification is not the intended purpose of the feedback process. In addition, a recipient of feedback will sometimes engage in the interchange more to please the giver than for his or her own benefit. If the process is to be effective, the receivers should be seriously concerned with receiving feedback and the senders should be legitimately interested in helping the receivers understand themselves by providing insights into their behavior.

6) *Give feedback at the time the behavior takes place.* As suggested earlier, feedback is most appropriately given immediately after behavior takes place (unless, of course, the receiver is personally unable to deal with feedback at that time). For example, if a sales manager says to a salesperson, "I observed you closing a sale with Mr. Jones last month, and you did not speak to him correctly," the details of the event are likely to have been long forgotten. Instead, if immediately after the incident the sales manager says, "You said to Mr. Jones, 'If you are a good businessman, you will buy this product,' instead of describing how the product would make his job easier or more effective," then the salesperson easily can check this information with his own perception of his performance and make a judgment about changing behavior.

7) *Give feedback when its accuracy can be checked with others.* It is useful to give feedback when others are present, so they can confirm the perceptions of the sender and demonstrate their accuracy to the receiver. For example, the author observed a meeting in which the president of a small manufacturing company was discussing his difficulty in getting information from his subordinates, ten of whom were present at the time. The president said, "No one tells me what is going on around here. A few people stop by my office but I do not see a lot of pantywaists for weeks at a time." At the close of the meeting, the author commented to the president that he had used a number of rather critical labels in describing his people, such as "pantywaists." The president reacted strongly saying, "What do you mean? I did not say 'pantywaist.' That word is not in my vocabulary. You are absolutely wrong." The author then said, turning to the ten subordinates, "How many people heard the president use that word?" and every hand in the room was raised (except for the president's). The strong confirmation of such feedback made it difficult for the president to deny his action, and he was forced to confront his behavior as it actually was, not as he might have wished it to be.

MAKING FACTUAL JUDGMENTS: COMPARED TO WHAT?

Thus far in our discussion, we have suggested that judgments tend to interfere with problem solving, yet it is apparent that one cannot avoid the words "good," "bad," "effective," "ineffective," "better," or "worse." As we shall see, if judgments are used in a certain way, problem-solving potential may actually increase. Two questions will help remind the reader of positive approaches. The first question is "Compared to what?" The second question is "How is it measured?" When used factually, a judgment compares something with something else. This something else may be one of several things: It may be a universal standard which everyone agrees is appropriate; it may be an a priori standard set before judgment of the behavior that takes place; it may be a comparison with prior behavior; or it may be a comparison with some other reference individual or group. Suppose, for example, Supervisor X tells Employee Y that his production last week was poor. Employee Y may respond, "Compared to what?" Given the alternatives suggested above, Supervisor X may respond, "We all know that the standard output for a professional in your job is 60 units per hour. You have been averaging 40," or "We both agreed last month that an acceptable level of performance for you in your job would be 60 units. You have been performing at a 40-unit level." Alternatively, the supervisor might observe, "You have been producing at 60 units per hour in your job for the last six months, but last week your production dropped to 40 units." Finally, the supervisor might state, "Employees A, B, and C are doing exactly the same kind of work as you, but they each average 60 units per hour compared to your average of 40 units per hour." It is, of course, desirable to establish bases of comparison prior to the situation in which behavior is judged, but it should be clear that nothing is good or bad in the absolute, only when it is compared to a standard.

Related to this issue is the matter of establishing multiple and detailed criteria whenever possible. Many emotional arguments can be turned into problem-solving issues if the parties can agree upon measures to be used for comparison and for judgment. For example, let us consider a college football team. Its fans may argue that it is a good or a bad team, to which one may respond, "Compared to what?" If the team has lost all of its games, it seems reasonable to say that it has not lived up to a universally accepted standard. If an announcement were made at the beginning of the season that the team would win half of its games, then it has not lived up to an a priori goal. If, in past years the team won half of its games and it has won none this year, then comparison with past performance indicates that it is less effective, or if it is at the bottom of the standings for teams in the league then it is not performing as well as other teams. But one may go further than this performance measure and seek other, more detailed standards. For example, team performance may be classified as physical or mental, as indicated in Figure 3-3. Physical factors might be further broken down into size and condition, mental factors into knowledge and attitudes, and these categories in turn may be further subdivided. Thus, in a discussion of whether the team is good or bad, one may compare the team with universal standards; a priori goals; past records; or other, more specific, standards of reference.

This same logic is used to determine the relative value of jobs for purposes of employee compensation through a process known as job evaluation. Instead of merely saying that Job A is more important than Job B, job evaluation systems break down jobs into knowledge requirement, physical effort, mental effort, etc., and rate jobs according

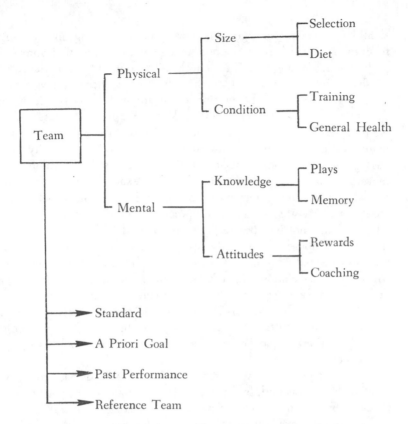

FIGURE 3–3.   Team Performance and Judgmental Standards.

to these criteria. Identical logic is used in systems of employee appraisal. Instead of saying that Employee A did a better job than Employee B, the two Employees are compared on the basis of production output, production quality, cost savings, time standards, and the like. To ask for the basis of comparison when a judgment is made will help to avoid conflict and will enhance the formation of judgments conducive to problem solving.

WHAT I HEARD YOU SAY WAS . . .

If one tries to keep communications at the Adult level, observes the rules for feedback, and identifies the basis for his judgments, one should find oneself engaging in more problem solving and less argumentation. A further admonition to one who wishes to improve his problem-solving language is to "check things out." Our experience tells us that what we say is not always what people hear and vice versa. Even when we try to be precise, there are many words which lend themselves to various interpretations. When we try to express feelings, we find that there are no exact words to describe them and that it takes many words to try and express our intent. Another difficulty is the passage of verbal communication through many screens and filters in movement from one person to another. For example, when the author was a graduate student moving from student housing into a better apartment, he was visited while in the process of moving by a chiropractor whom he had not met before. The author said, "My family and I are moving to a house by degrees," meaning one step at a time. The chiropractor answered, "I'm always learning myself." The word *degrees* had triggered an association with education in the mind of the chiropractor (who may have been sensitive to the issue because of constant comparison between chiropractors and physicians). In any case, we need no theoretical model to tell us that the disparity between what people say and what other people hear is the source of many problems of communication.

This problem may be resolved if Party X feeds back to Party Y what X thinks was said, by simply saying, "What I heard you say was," followed by a summary of the message received.

A good exercise in this regard is for two people to conduct a conversation with the condition that the receiver of a communication cannot respond until he has summarized what he heard to the satisfaction of the sender. The exercise enhances listening skills and clarifies the extent to which verbal messages can be fashioned to minimize the likelihood of their being misunderstood. This exercise also enhances skills in conducting a dialogue instead of an interaction often likened to a ping-pong game. The ping-pong game metaphor works in the following fashion: A makes a statement but B does not really listen to it, since B is simply letting A finish so that B can express his thoughts (uninterrupted by A's statement). Similarly, A does not listen to B but rather waits for him to finish so A can send his own message, and so on back and forth. There is a story which further exemplifies our point in which George says to Sam, "My wife just had a baby." Sam responds, "My wife just bought a new car." George says, "It's a girl." Sam says, "It's blue."

It was stated that for problem solving to take place, both

parties must have the same information. This applies not only to production figures or financial data but also to what is going on in each person's head—cognitive and emotional processes. As we shall see later, it is not necessary that both parties agree, but simply that they understand each other as completely as possible. In this chapter we have talked primarily about verbal communication. Later we shall discuss nonverbal messages.

NOTE ON EXPERIENTIAL LEARNING

Exercise 3 in the Appendix, "Individual Leveling and Feedback," and Exercise 4, "Giving and Receiving Help and Feedback," both utilize the methodology described in this chapter. Exercise 3 is most useful in eliciting comparisons between how people see themselves and how others see them. Exercise 4 is particularly useful in the development of problem-solving and consultative skills.

Exercise 5 in the Appendix, "Individual Characteristics and Occupation," will illustrate the extent to which group members have stereotypes. Such stereotypes are part of the Parent mode in the transactional-analysis model discussed in this chapter.

REFERENCES

Berne, E. *Transactional Analysis in Psychotherapy.* Grove, 1961.

Frankl, V. E. *Man's Search for Meaning: An Introduction to Logotherapy.* Beacon, 1959.

Harris, T. *I'm OK, You're OK: A Practical Guide to Transactional Analysis.* Harper & Row, 1969.

Luft, J. "The Johari Window." *Human Relations Training News* 5 (1961): 6–7.

National Training Laboratories' Summer Reading Book (Bethel, Maine). NTL Institute for Applied Behavioral Science, 1968.

Personal Styles of   4
Conflict Resolution

People learn behavior in different ways. Much learning occurs through trial and error as an individual discovers that one behavior leads to reward or pleasure and another behavior leads to punishment or pain. People also learn behavior by patterning themselves after models. One individual behaves like another because the other seems to have gained reward or satisfaction through a particular behavioral style. Still another method for learning calls for the individual to make a conscious choice regarding behavior. This process involves establishing possible alternative behaviors, determining the likely consequences of those behaviors, computing the odds that the costs or benefits associated with the different behaviors will actually take place, and selection of the best behavior.

The effect of these different methods of learning on supervisory training is illustrated in a study by Couch (1965), who compared incidents from which two groups of supervisors reported that they learned supervisory techniques. One group had a high degree of training related to supervisory practices; the other group had little or no training in such practices. Both groups, it should be pointed out, had the same degree of overall education. Couch's results indicated that both groups learned principally through personal experience. However, the well-trained group learned by reasoning processes and by observation, while the poorly trained group learned by trial and error. The well-trained group gained information from peers, subordinates, and superiors, while the poorly trained group often simply imitated the behavior of an immediate superior. Thus, supervisory training apparently gave the well-trained group the means to analyze information gained through their own experience.

Regardless of the source of learning, however, behavior eventually becomes fixed and resistant to change; once we are comfortable with a pattern of behavior, there are costs associated with changing a practiced and familiar style. A different style is unfamiliar, perhaps uncomfortable, and might lead to unpredictable outcomes. This chapter focuses on the patterns of behavior which individuals utilize for conflict resolution and provides a model for analyzing the consequences of different styles.[1] In a later chapter we shall address the problem of changing one's pattern of behavior.

STYLES OF CONFLICT

As the axes in Figure 4–1 indicate, there are at least two major concerns in a conflict situation. One concern involves the extent to which an individual wishes to meet his own personal goals. In the present discussion we shall take *goals* to mean either *means* or *ends*, since a person may see his goal as that of doing the task the way he wants to do it or of accomplishing an end which he personally values. Another concern is the extent to which an individual wants to maintain a relationship with another individual or group and to be accepted by that individual or group. For the sake of convenience, in Figure 4–1 concern for personal goals is scaled from 1 to 9, representing the increasing degree of importance in the mind of the individual; similarly, concern for relationships is scaled from 1 (low concern) to 9 (high concern). Given this scaling, we may identify the following approximate types or styles: High concern for personal goals and low concern for relationships (9,1); low concern for personal goals and high concern for relationships (1,9); low concern for personal goals and low con-

1. *This chapter is based on Robert R. Blake and Jane S. Mouton, "The Fifth Achievement,"* The Journal of Applied Behavioral Science, *Vol. 6, No. 4, 1970, pp. 413–26 and Jay Hall,* Conflict Management Survey, *Houston, Texas: Teleometrics, Inc., 1969.*

FIGURE 4–1.   A Model of Conflict Management Styles. Special permission for reproduction of the material below is granted by the author, Jay Hall, Ph.D., and publisher, Teleometrics International. All rights reserved and no reproductions should be made without express approval of Teleometrics International.

Concern for Relationship

9

1/9

Differences only serve to drive people apart; their "personal" implications cannot be ignored. Realistically, to differ is to reject. Maximum attention to the needs and desires of others is required if relationships are to endure. Conflict requires self-sacrifice and placing the importance of continued relationships above one's own goals. It is better to ignore differences than to risk open combat by being oversensitive; one must guard against causing irreparable damage to his relationships.

9/9

Differences are a natural part of the human condition. In and of themselves, they are neither good nor bad. Conflict is usually a symptom of tensions in relationships, and should be treated accordingly. When accurately interpreted, they may be resolved and serve to strengthen relationships, rather than to divide. Conflict requires confrontation and objective problem solving, often of a type that goes beyond the apparent needs and opinions of the parties involved. Not only are people brought more closely together when conflicts are worked through, but creativity may be achieved as well.

5/5

Differences should be treated in the light of the common good. At times some parties are obliged to lay aside their own views in the interest of the majority; this allows the relationship to continue to function, however imperfectly, and affords a basis for redress later on. Everyone should have an opportunity to air his views and feelings, but these should not be allowed to block progress. It is never possible for everyone to be satisfied and those who insist on such an unrealistic goal should be shown the error of their way. Resolution requires a good deal of skill and persuasive ability coupled with flexibility.

1/1

Differences simply reflect the more basic attributes which distinguish among people: past experiences, irrational needs, innate limitations and potentials and levels of personal aspirations. As such, they are essentially beyond the influence of others. They constitute necessary evils in human affairs, and one must either accept them or withdraw from human contacts. Impersonal tolerance is the most enlightened approach to handling conflicts.

9/1

Differences are to be expected among people for they reflect the nature of the species: some have skills and others have none, and some are right and some are wrong. Ultimately right prevails, and this is the central issue in conflict. One owes it to himself and those who rely on his judgment to prevail in conflicts with others whose opinions and goals are in doubt. Persuasion, power, and force are all acceptable tools for achieving conflict resolution; and most people expect them to be employed.

1

9

Concern for Personal Goals

cern for relationships (1,1); moderate concern for personal goals and moderate concern for relationships (5,5); and high concern for personal goals and high concern for relationships (9,9). Let us consider each style.

The (9,1) win-lose style—"the tough battler"

One who seeks to meet his own goals at all costs, without concern for the needs or the acceptance of others, engages in tough battles. For such an individual, winning or losing is not merely an event; instead, he views losing as reduced status, weakness, and the loss of his self-image. On the other hand, to win gives the (9,1) person a sense of exhilaration and achievement. There is no doubt in his mind that he is right; he stands by his convictions and defends his position, expressing anger and frustration when others do not accede to him. He feels that if there is a winner there must be a loser and that he must be the winner, whatever the cost. The (9,1) person is quite willing to sacrifice individuals in a group if they refuse to go along with his desires. For him, conflict is a nuisance which occurs only because others do not see the correctness of his own position. He demonstrates to those with whom he disagrees that they are wrong with facts that support his own position.

The (1,9) yield-lose style—"the friendly helper"

This type of person overvalues maintenance of relationships with others and undervalues achievement of his own goals. He desires acceptance by others and gives in to their desires where they are in conflict with his own. He is the kind of person who might say, "Well, yes, there are some things I would like to have accomplished, but it's OK, I don't want to make trouble." He feels differences can't be discussed or confronted to any extent without someone getting hurt in the process. Conflict, he feels, grows out of the self-centeredness of individuals and should be avoided in favor of harmony. He seems to feel that anger is bad and that confrontation is destructive; he may try to redirect potential conflict by breaking the tension with humor or suggesting some nonconflictive activity. Mutuality of interests and harmony of relationships are paramount in his approach.

The (1,1) lose-leave style

The person using this style sees conflict as a hopeless, useless, and punishing experience. Rather than undergo the tension and frustration of conflict, the person using the (1,1) style simply removes himself either mentally or physically. Encounters with others are kept as impersonal as possible, and in case of disagreement, the (1,1) person will withdraw. He will comply to avoid disagreement and tension, will feel little commitment to the decision reached, and will not openly take sides in a disagreement among others.

The (5,5) compromise style

The basis of this approach is that half a loaf is better than none. One using this style seeks to find a position which allows each side to gain something. The (5,5) person enjoys the maneuvering required to resolve conflict and will actively seek to find some strong middle ground between two extreme positions. He may vacillate between expressing anger and then trying to smooth things over, and may seek to use voting or rules as a way of avoiding direct confrontation on the issues. If he is confronted with a serious disagreement, he will suggest some mechanism for finding a "workable" solution (such as voting or trading) rather than working out the disagreement in order to find the best solution.

The (9,9) integrative style—"the problem solver"

The individual employing the (9,9) style actively seeks to satisfy his own goals as well as the goals of others. The (9,9) person does not see the two sets of objectives as mutually exclusive and feels that no one's goals need be sacrificed if the appropriate conflict resolution is achieved. The (9,9) person (1) sees conflict as natural and helpful, even leading to a more creative solution if handled properly; (2) evidences trust and candidness with others and recognizes the legitimacy of feelings in arriving at decisions; (3) feels that the attitudes and positions of everyone need to be aired and recognizes that when conflict is resolved to the satisfaction of all, commitment to the solution is likely; (4) sees everyone as having an equal role in resolving the conflict, views the opinions of everyone as equally legitimate; and (5) does not sacrifice anyone simply for the good of the group.

RELATIONSHIP OF CONFLICT STYLES AND OTHER RESEARCH

As just described, Hall (1969) has identified five different behavior styles. Of these five, we shall consider the three which research describes in more detail. They are: (1) the "tough battler," who seeks his own goals and is willing to sacrifice the goals of others; (2) the "friendly helper," who gives in to the goals of others even at the cost of his own desires; and (3) the "problem solver," who seeks to find an outcome that meets both his goals and the goals of others.

Bargaining styles similar to these three have recently been investigated by Cummings and his associates (Cummings et al., 1971; Harnett et al., 1973). They adapted a scale developed to measure personality and attitudes in experimental bargaining situations originated by Shure and Meeker (1965) and correlated the three bargaining styles with four dimensions from the Shure-Meeker questionnaire (Cummings et al., 1972). The personality dimensions in the questionnaire are as follows:

1) Conciliation versus belligerence in interpersonal relations. Conciliators advocate responding to the needy or less fortunate with understanding, help, and friendliness. They admit their own wrongs and are not motivated by revenge.

2) Risk avoidance versus risk taking. Risk avoiders are unadventurous, have a low activity level, and will not expose themselves to dangers or hazardous risks.

3) External versus internal control. Externally controlled persons believe that events are controlled by external forces over which they have no control; that is, by fate or chance.

4) Suspiciousness versus trust. Suspicious persons are characterized by quasi-paranoid traits of selfishness, projection of hostility, excitability, tenseness, and the lack of trust.

By combining these personality dimensions with various forms of bargaining behavior, we are able to present a typology of such behaviors and the personality correlates of each. Cummings and his associates identified three types of bargainers, the "tough bargainer," the "soft bargainer," and the "equalizer." For our purposes, the "tough bargainer" is equivalent to what we have called the "tough battler" (9,1); the "soft bargainer" is our "friendly helper" (1,9); and the "equalizer" is our "problem solver" (9,9). These three bargaining styles, it will be noted, also exhibit similarities to the Parent, Adult, and Child behaviors described in Chapter 3.

Cummings and his associates found that "tough bargainers" were high in internal control, risk taking, and belligerence. The style is unrelated to measures of trust or suspiciousness. The relationships are quite consistent with those posited for the win-lose battlers, since they believe strongly in their own rightness and will do almost anything to avoid losing the battle and destroying their egos.

The win-lose battling style is also consistent with the "Parent" behavior of the transactional analysis model proposed by Eric Berne (1961). The Parent is normative, controlling, and judgmental in his statements and behavior. Like the win-lose battler, he makes sharp distinctions between right and wrong and is unconcerned with the gray area between the two extremes. The Parent thinks in terms of fixed rules and values and will probably elicit either Parent behavior (counterdependence) or Child behavior (dependence) from those with whom he or she interacts.

The second style to be considered is the helping or yielding approach. The soft bargainer actively seeks acceptance and affiliation with others, and maintains relationships by yielding to the demands or goals of others, since he feels that interpersonal relations are too fragile to withstand direct confrontations on differences. Such a person complies with the wishes of others at the cost of personal goals.

The Cummings data indicate that the soft bargainer is high in external control, low in risk taking, and high in trust. The style is unrelated to conciliation or belligerence. Thus, the soft bargainer might be expected to give in to the demands of others and to avoid the risks of damaging interpersonal relationships. Trust and optimism may help to make this dependent position more tenable.

The soft style reminds us of the "Child" behavior in the transactional analysis model. The Child is subordinate, dependent, and characterized by emotionalism and fantasy. This orientation is certainly antithetical to conflict resolution based on mutual understanding of facts and mutual respect for the needs of others.

The third style to be considered is that of the problem solver, which Hall calls "the dominant style for conflict management." The problem solver believes that his goals and the goals of others are not mutually exclusive, and seeks to maintain the relationship and to meet his own goals by searching for solutions which are mutually acceptable. He believes that more can be achieved with two parties working together than when a single party dominates, and acknowledges the reality of facts and feelings as a necessary ingredient for the resolution of conflict. He deals with others in a trusting, open, and candid way.

There is a problem-solving style, identified by Cummings as that of the "equalizer," which is fact-oriented rather than defeat-oriented and which seeks a fair outcome for both parties. The equalizer is found to be high in internal control, high in trusting behavior, high in conciliation, and unrelated to the measure of risk taking: Other research (Zand, 1972) has shown that trusting behavior is displayed when one does not avoid stating facts, ideas, or feelings that might make him vulnerable to others. One exhibiting trusting behavior does not resist or deflect attempts of others to exert control over him and is responsive to their suggestions. That is, he can work interdependently with others rather than seeking to dominate or to control.

The problem solver is explicitly associated with the "Adult" style in the transactional analysis model. The Adult deals with facts and reality, does not dominate or impose arbitrary rules as does the Parent, and is not involved in fantasy as is the Child. The Adult deals with a problem descriptively and concentrates on giving and receiving information. There is no automatic right or wrong or good or bad but, rather, a need to solve problems objectively.

THE INTERACTION OF DIFFERENT STYLES

The bargaining literature (Cummings et al., 1971) also provides information about the consequences when pairs of different styles interact with each other. Again, we shall focus upon the tough bargainer (or win-lose battler), the soft bargainer (or friendly helper), and the equalizer (or problem solver). As indicated in Table 4–1, the

TABLE 4–1.   Estimated Outcomes in Dyadic Combinations of Conflict Style in Bargaining. Courtesy, Larry L. Cummings, University of Wisconsin.

	Win-lose battler	Friendly helper	Problem solver
Win-lose battler	Stalemate 80%	Battler wins 90%	Battler wins over 50%
Friendly helper	X	Stalemate 80%	Problem solver wins
Problem solver	X	X	Quick agreement

confrontation between two tough battlers most frequently results in a stalemate. As might be expected, the battler dealing with a friendly helper is expected to be the winner; when interacting with the problem solver, the battler wins over 50 percent of the time. Curiously, when two friendly helpers face each other, a stalemate frequently results; when a friendly helper deals with a problem solver, the latter typically wins. Problem solvers interacting with each other deal factually with a perceived problem and arrive quickly at an agreeable solution.

The bargaining literature also suggests what style of conflict resolution is more practical. We might ask whether the problem-solving style is really better on objective grounds, that is, "in the real world." If by "objective" we mean whether or not an agreement is actually reached and whether or not the agreement provides advantages relative to the possible agreements obtained through the use of the other styles, then clearly the problem-solving style is favored.

USING DIFFERENT STYLES

As we indicated in Chapter 2, effective conflict resolvers rely heavily upon problem solving (9,9) and smoothing (1,9). On the other hand, ineffective conflict resolvers rely upon forcing (9,1) and withdrawal (1,1). Compromise can be used in both effective and ineffective ways. An explanation for these differences in conflict-resolving techniques may lie in the parties' beliefs about whether or not agreement or a mutually beneficial solution is possible. Blake, Mouton, and Shepard (1964) suggest that when the parties believe that agreement is possible and the stakes are high, they will engage in problem solving; on the other hand, if the stakes are low and the consequences of the outcome are not particularly important, they will smooth over the disagreement, yielding if necessary.

In contrast, when the parties do not believe that agreement is possible and the stakes are high, they will engage in win-lose strategies. A party's behavior in this case represents the attitude, "Well, someone has to lose and it isn't going to be me." When the stakes are low, on the other hand, the parties will simply be inactive and leave the outcome to fate. Thus, the behavior which parties exhibit in a situation depends upon several variables: (1) each party's beliefs about the possibility of arriving at an agreement, (2) the objective possibility of finding a win-win solution, and (3) the relative consequences for each party if either or both cannot find a satisfactory solution.

An important element determining whether the parties believe that a mutually acceptable solution is possible is the knowledge of how to arrive at mutually acceptable, integrative solutions. As we pointed out earlier, people will more than likely persist in using methods which are not particularly effective just because they have used them before.

The particular style which *should* be used in a given conflict situation must, of course, depend upon the measures of goodness involved. We have suggested that the problem-solving or integrative style has certain benefits which may make it most desirable. It enhances creativity, promotes understanding, increases the likelihood that both parties will be objectively and subjectively satisfied with the outcome, and provides an aftermath which promotes further trust and cooperation. But it is also time-consuming in most cases and, thus, can be an expensive method. One should have the capacity to use all conflict-resolving styles and to know when they can most effectively be used. Said another way, the styles of conflict resolution are tools—not ends in themselves. They are not particularly good or bad except insofar as they accomplish particular objectives.

Viewed from the perspective discussed above, the tough (9,1) style may be seen either as an end in itself or as a tool. An individual using the (9,1) style as an end says simply that it is "best." An individual using the tough style as a tool says, "These are my objectives and given the likely consequences of using various styles, I will select the tough (9,1) style." For example, if one's objective is to defeat the other party, then one might select the (9,1) style and try to use it as skillfully as possible. Similarly, under certain circumstances, a father or mother might choose to dominate and control small children, in spite of the feelings or attitudes of the children.

In the same way, the helping (1,9) style may be seen either as an end in itself or as a tool. If an individual treats the helping style as an end, that individual is saying that yielding is good, avoiding conflict is good, and/or helping others is good. On the other hand, the helping style, used as a tool, simply leads to certain outcomes which must be evaluated before an individual can decide whether it is best to use this style. For example, a manager may accede to his employees' wishes for a change in working hours because the desire for harmonious relations outweighs the minor inconvenience to himself and because the stakes are so low that problem solving is not warranted.

Finally, the compromise (5,5) style may be seen either as an end in itself or as a tool. Coming about through application of a company's policies and rules, compromise is seen as an end when members of the organization behave out of simple obedience to those policies. In contrast, when the members of an organization say, "The policies and rules of this organization are merely means to certain ends," they view compromise as a tool. An organization's rules are like the traffic signals at busy intersections, they provide predictability of behavior and coordination of effort.

In sum, each of the styles of conflict resolution may be appropriate in different circumstances. Proper conflict-resolving behavior is based on having the skills required for each style and on knowing when each style can most effectively be used.

NOTE ON EXPERIENTIAL LEARNING

A measurement of the personal conflict resolution styles discussed in this chapter has been developed by Jay Hall. The scale measures the extent to which the respondent uses each of the five styles mentioned—win-lose, yield-lose, lose-leave, compromise, and integrative —in hypothetical conflict situations. The survey also measures the extent to which the styles are used in person-to-person conflicts, intragroup conflicts, and intergroup conflicts. The reader may obtain this useful tool by ordering *Conflict Management Survey,* Teleometrics International, P.O. Drawer 1850, Conroe, Texas 77301.

REFERENCES

Berne, E. *Transactional Analysis in Psychotherapy.* Grove, 1961.

Blake, R. R., and J. S. Mouton. "The fifth achievement." *Journal of Applied Behavioral Science* 6 (1970): 413–26.

Blake, R. R., J. S. Mouton, and H. A. Shepard. *Managing Intergroup Conflict in Industry.* Gulf, 1964.

Couch, P. D. "Some effects of training and experience on concepts of supervision." Unpublished doctoral dissertation, University of Wisconsin-Madison, 1965.

Cummings, L. L., D. L. Harnett, and O. J. Stevens. "Risk, fate, conciliation and trust; An international study of attitudinal differences among executives." *Academy of Management Journal* 14 (1971): 285–304.

Cummings, L. L., D. L. Harnett, and S. M. Schmidt. "International cross-language factor stability of personality: An analysis of the Shure-Meeker Personality/Attitude Schedule." *The Journal of Psychology* 82 (1972): 67–84.

Hall, J. *Conflict Management Survey*. Teleometrics, 1969.

Harnett, D. L., L. L. Cummings, and W. C. Hamner. "Personality, bargaining style, and payoff in bilateral monopoly bargaining among European managers." *Sociometry* 36 (1973): 325–45.

Shure, G. H., R. J. Meeker, and E. A. Hansford. "The effectiveness of pacifist strategies in bargaining games." *The Journal of Conflict Resolution* 9 (1965): 106–17.

Zand, D. E. "Trust and managerial problem solving." *Administrative Science Quarterly* 17 (1972): 229–39.

Attitudes and
Problem Solving

5

In this chapter, we shall identify attitudes associated with the win-win method (problem-solving method) rather than with win-lose or lose-lose methods. The belief system within individuals strongly affects whether they engage in attempts to arrive at consensus or whether they choose instead to do battle with opponents. For example, if Party A mistrusts Party B in a potential conflict situation, it is unlikely that A will share information freely with B and disclose personal feelings. Party B will react to this mistrust by behaving aggressively or defensively, and the energy of both parties will be directed toward battling the other rather than attacking the problem itself.

BELIEFS CONDUCIVE TO PROBLEM SOLVING

A number of predisposing attitudes are associated with the use of problem-solving and consensus methods; all of these attitudes derive from central concepts of cooperation and trust.

BELIEF IN THE AVAILABILITY OF A MUTUALLY ACCEPTABLE SOLUTION

Perhaps the most important requisite for consensus is an optimistic rather than a pessimistic view about the possibility of arriving at a mutually acceptable solution to a problem. Problem solving can be a frustrating and time-consuming process. Unless both parties believe that a mutually acceptable solution exists, each will compromise his position or seek a win-lose solution. It should be reemphasized that the method which we are developing in this book shifts attention from means to ends, and finds the pooling of different objectives quite appropriate. When parties argue about "my way versus your way," they have in fact skipped the essential step in problem solving—a definition of goals. That is, if the goals are defined, the parties can then proceed to find a different way or a new alternative that satisfies the needs of both. The process does not imply that both parties must necessarily seek the same objective. Rather, it holds that a solution exists which achieves everyone's goals.

Perhaps an analogy will help clarify the issue. Many people's beliefs about trust are illustrated in the statement "I will not trust you until you prove to me that you can be trusted." An individual's expression of these cues indicating lack of trust makes it difficult for another individual to respond in a positive way. However, when an individual starts with the premise "I will trust you until you prove that I should do otherwise," the likelihood of establishing mutual trust is far greater. Thus, in like manner, saying "I believe we can find a mutually acceptable solution unless it is proved otherwise" is much more likely to be functional than saying "I won't believe that we can find a mutually acceptable solution until you demonstrate to me that we can."

BELIEF IN THE DESIRABILITY OF A MUTUALLY ACCEPTABLE SOLUTION

The focus of problem solving is upon a superordinate goal. The parties involved are saying, in effect, "We will have succeeded when we solve the problem in a manner which meets the needs of all parties and is not unacceptable to anyone."

The practical value of belief in the desirability of a mutually acceptable solution is suggested by the fact that while the joint or group decision will take longer to achieve than an individual decision, the joint decision increases the likelihood of support for and understanding of the final solution by all parties (Maier, 1970). Where implementation of a decision depends upon acceptance by some of the parties, then the needs of those parties must be considered in making the decision.

For example, the management of a manufacturing company may be interested in minimizing its inventory of raw materials in order to use the money invested in such materials for other purposes. There are, of course, a variety of solutions to such a problem—including manual or computer records, segmenting inventory into reorder points and individual item control, and assignment of responsibility to supervisory or staff personnel. Production personnel (whose understanding and support is needed to make the system work) may be interested in avoiding inconveniences, maintaining a smooth flow of production, and avoiding delays which affect personal earnings. Problem solving by management and production personnel should yield a system which is beneficial to both.

In addition to maximizing acceptance and understanding, the process of finding a mutually acceptable, high quality decision through joint decision making also increases the likelihood of finding a solution that is better than one achieved through individual decision making. Research indicates that for many kinds of problems or judgments, group decisions are either as good as or better than the best individual judgment in a group (Shaw, 1971).

Both the belief that a mutually acceptable goal can be achieved and a demonstration of the desirability of achieving such a goal are enhanced by the successful application of integrative decision making (IDM). Successful experiential exercises (like those included in the appendix of this book) help one to develop these beliefs in a controlled setting. In such cases, a facilitator or trainer helps people acquire new beliefs and practice new skills, thus building facility and assurance in the trainees in much the same way a tennis coach will help an individual unlearn poor skills and acquire new skills by demonstration and practice on the tennis court. Little would be gained by merely talking about tennis in the classroom; practice and success are required with new behavior in the actual performance situation before real progress can be made.

BELIEF IN COOPERATION RATHER THAN COMPETITION

The belief that competitive behavior is good and desirable is deep-seated in many cultures, especially in our own. We are taught that good boys and girls compete and that the best win in such competition. All too often, such processes become self-justifying and generalized. For example, a leader may be viewed as superior and best able to lead by virtue of winning the competition for the leadership position. The leader's power may then be generalized if those influenced by it say to themselves, "Well, X was superior in the task which determined leadership; therefore, X must be superior in many other things, too." Other examples of this phenomenon are to be found in companies that promote successful salespeople to managerial positions and universities that move professors who teach well into administrative posts. In both cases, success in the new job is not assured merely because the individual performed an entirely different job well, yet that success has been generalized into an assumption that the individuals can carry out *any* task.

The ethic of competition derives from a misinterpretation of Darwin's notion of survival of the fittest. Many believe that Darwin postulated a situation in which individuals or groups compete with each other, and the fittest, that is, those who are superior or strongest, win while those who are inferior lose. In fact, however, Darwin postulated man's competition with nature and subsequent adaptation for purposes of physical survival. Those who would adjust to the demands of the environment would continue to exist, while those who could not adjust would perish. It is argued here that man can best adjust to his environment through cooperation, rather than through competition, with his fellows.

There is a great deal of consistent evidence to suggest that cooperative groups are more satisfied, have greater interest in the task, are more productive, and have a better division of labor than competitive groups. The last point should be noted particularly. To illustrate: If five men are engaged in the task of climbing a mountain and are competing, each must depend upon his own knowledge of the task, physical skill, and strength in carrying his equipment. It is not likely that group members will share information about the task with each other. In a cooperative group, on the other hand, tasks can be allocated among group members according to their skills and interests. One member may have superior knowledge about the process of preparation and may lead in the planning effort; another may have superior skill in mountain climbing and may lead in that activity; another may have much greater physical strength than the others and may carry a greater load up the mountain. Thus, cooperation can fully utilize the unique strengths and skills of each member and can foster sharing of resources within the group.

It may be argued that intergroup competition will strengthen performance and increase cohesiveness within each individual group, and indeed, this does happen; yet after a competition between two groups, only the winning group is likely to remain cohesive and satisfied. The defeated group will become fragmented and dissatisfied, perhaps seeking an opportunity for retaliation. There are cases, however, where defeat can also unify a group, but they are largely limited to (1) those cases in which the group perceives its defeat as the result of some negative influence or something completely outside its control, or (2) cases where the group competes frequently, and the winning/ losing positions shift regularly.

Since competition between groups may have a positive effect upon the task interest and satisfaction within the groups, one might well conclude that one could benefit from its useful effects so long as competition is not ended, and the parties do not polarize into winners and losers. For example, a manager might reason, "I shall keep two departments in competition with each other without ever letting the competition terminate into winning and losing groups." However, for competition to have the functional effects mentioned above, each individual must see a connection between his behavior and an end result. If the individual does not see that connection, then the competitive situation ceases to be motivating. In much the same sense, direct incentive pay, linking behavior to immediate reward, may have positive effects on production. A profit-sharing plan in which present behavior is only ambiguously and distantly related to reward, however, will probably have little incentive effect on behavior.

Before leaving this issue, it should be noted that we are discussing relationships between individuals and groups generally within a single organization. We are not addressing the broader issue of competition among organizations in society. It may be plausibly argued that competition among business organizations fosters innovation and efficiency, which benefit the consumer by the development of new or cheaper products. Assuming this to be the case, we may conclude that although some good may derive from interorganizational competition, intraorganizational competition among people whose efforts are interdependent is not only inappropriate but also potentially destructive. Problem-solving groups are cooperative, and all group members benefit; competition is a win-lose method and creates more conflicts than it resolves.

BELIEF THAT EVERYONE IS OF EQUAL VALUE

Some differences among people make them valuable in a problem-solving activity. Different knowledge, different attitudes, different perspectives, and different abilities all add to the resources of a group. Such differences are givens, not to be judged right or wrong, good or bad, superior or inferior, acceptable or unacceptable.

On the other hand, differences in power or status which serve to separate the group into we-they factions are dysfunctional in problem solving. In a university committee, for example, where faculty members traditionally have status and power, student members often are restricted to a minority number to limit their voting power or even are restricted to nonvoting positions. Faculty members will say that the students do not have perspective or knowledge, ignoring the fact that they themselves do not have the knowledge or perspective that students have. Similarly, business managers frequently state that there is no point in giving workers informaton about company plans or finances, since they just would not understand the information. The latter example differs in degree, but not in kind, from that of the slave master saying, "The slaves cannot possibly think for themselves or work with us on an equal basis. They are like children and must be cared for."

The consequences of power differences and unequal status on organizational behavior can be seen in an analysis of attitude surveys. Factor analysis of survey results indicates that attitudes toward the company and attitudes toward its top management are the same in the minds of respondents; that is, workers feel the same way toward the company as they do toward top management. When status differences make employees hostile to top management, there is little wonder that an irate employee might say, "I will put forth a minimum effort for eight hours a day while working in *your* company (not in *our* company)."

BELIEF IN THE VIEWS OF OTHERS AS LEGITI-MATE STATEMENTS OF THEIR POSITION

IDM requires that each individual accept the knowledge, attitudes, and theories of others as data to be included in the problem-solving process. If A judges B's statements to be wrong or inappropriate,

B may react with feelings of threat or defensiveness. Similarly, if A tries to persuade B that the latter's feelings are not correct, it is unlikely that B's belief system will actually change. There is some information, of course, which is purely objective and unconnected to the sentiments or values held by B. In these cases information is merely added to B's knowledge. Most information, however, does affect one's belief system, and here it is safe to say that one changes oneself, rather than being changed by others.

In IDM one takes the information gained from others in the problem-solving process as an accurate and true statement of their position. One also fully accepts a change in that position. If I say to you, "An hour ago you stated a belief that is inconsistent with what you are saying now," I merely punish your growth and development and defeat a movement toward problem solving. Therapeutic experience also suggests that when an individual's views are accepted and believed without judgment, he can more easily change them when confronted with contradictory information.

This notion of acceptance is subtle but important. One cannot merely say to oneself, "OK, I will accept what he says," if one still harbors judgments against the other's views. Recalling the transactional analysis model we discussed in Chapter 3, if a person establishes an arbitrary rule for himself to behave in an accepting and understanding way and to ignore his own latent feelings, he is operating as a Parent; but when an individual objectively behaves as a witness and information gatherer, he is within the problem-solving mode of the Adult. Perhaps some comments by Carl Rogers will help to make this notion clear:

> . . . I find that the more accepting and liking I feel toward this individual, the more I will be creating a relationship which he can use. By acceptance I mean a warm regard for him as a person of unconditional self worth—of value no matter what his condition, his behavior or his feelings. It means a respect and liking for him as a separate person, a willingness for him to possess his own feelings in his own way. It means an acceptance of and regard for his attitudes of the moment, no matter how negative or positive, no matter how much they may contradict other attitudes he has held in the past . . . acceptance does not mean much until it involves understanding. It is not as I *understand* the feelings and thoughts which seem so horrible to you or so weak or so sentimental or so bizarre—it is only as I see them as you see them and accept

them and you that you feel really free to explore all the hidden nooks and frightening crannies of your inner and often buried experience. This *freedom* is an important condition of the relationship. (Rogers, 1961, p. 34)

However, it must be pointed out that acceptance does not necessarily mean agreement. To say, "I understand your position and accept your statements as what you believe," does not also mean I must agree with your statements. In this sense my position is different from yours, not better, not worse, just different. If a child is afraid of the dark, one does not say, "You are wrong," or, "I am better than you are because I am not afraid of the dark." Instead, one attempts to understand that fear and perhaps convey to the child one's own experiences with darkness. Then, if the child does not change his own attitudes, one attempts to deal with the problem.

BELIEF THAT DIFFERENCES OF OPINION ARE HELPFUL

Disagreement frequently leads to creativity in problem solving as long as it does not disrupt the group process. Consider, for example, the case described in Chapter 2 in which prison officials argued about whether or not to use uniforms for security personnel in a model prison. The majority of those present preferred not to use uniforms; the minority wished to do so. The discussion elicited the reasons for the positions held by each of the two groups. Further, when these needs were combined for purposes of defining the problem and the groups searched for new alternatives, they found a creative solution which satisfied the needs of everyone. The eventual result of this difference of opinion was the achievement of a new and unique system for identifying authority within the prison which dispelled the stereotypes associated with prison uniforms.

BELIEF IN TRUSTWORTHINESS OF OTHER MEMBERS

As suggested above, integrative decision making depends upon the belief that each member in the problem-solving situation can be trusted. *Trust* is defined behaviorally as "actions which increase one's vulnerability to another whose behavior is not under one's control in a situation in which the penalty one suffers, if the other abuses that vulnerability, is greater than the benefit one gains if the other does not abuse that vulnerability" (Zand, 1972, p. 230). For example, parents exhibit trust when they hire a baby-sitter so that they can see a movie, and a company president exhibits trust in subordinates when he tells them that he has been advised by the board of directors that his job depends on a significant improvement in the company's financial performance in the coming year.

As Zand suggests, one who trusts others will not conceal or distort relevant information and will not avoid stating facts, ideas, conclusions, and feelings that would make him vulnerable to others. He will neither resist nor deflect attempts of others to exert influence upon him, but will be responsive to their suggestions, at the same time not expecting them necessarily to accept his views. Moreover, one who trusts others is capable of depending upon them, feeling that he can rely on them to abide by agreements. He can accept their attempts to control his behavior when warranted by the situation; that is, he can work interdependently with others.

In a study comparing problem-solving groups—half of which were directed to trust other people, to express their views openly, to share information freely, and to aim at a high level of mutual confidence; and the other half directed to behave in opposite ways—Zand found support for the following hypotheses. Problem-solving groups with high trust will: (1) exchange relevant ideas and feelings more openly, (2) develop greater clarification of goals and problems, (3) search more extensively for alternative courses of action, (4) have greater influence on solutions, (5) be more satisfied with their problem-solving efforts, (6) have greater motivation to implement conclusions, (7) see themselves as closer and more of a team, and (8) have less desire to leave their group to join another. These differences were perceived both by members of problem-solving groups and by observers of those groups.

It seems likely that in Zand's study trusting behavior on the part of group members evoked, or at least confirmed, trusting behavior on the part of other group members. This suggests that where one gives evidence to others that he does not trust them, his distrustful cues will evoke distrustful behavior on their part. Conversely, trusting cues are likely to evoke trusting behavior from others. For this reason, it is better to assume that others can be trusted, and to change that view only in the light of specific evidence to the contrary, rather than to initially assume the opposite.

BELIEF THAT THE OTHER PARTY CAN COMPETE BUT CHOOSES TO COOPERATE

From what has been said so far, it appears that cooperation is a more effective group strategy than is competition. Yet the issue is far more complicated than this. For one thing, the actions of one party are not independent of the actions of another. Although one party may choose to cooperate, the viability of that choice depends upon the actions of the other party. Also, the extent to which the parties will continue to interact varies. If one party gains substantially at the other's expense in a single interaction, further interaction may be blocked by the loser, or continued only if an opportunity for retaliation is provided.

Some insights into this issue of the relative advantages of cooperation and competition may be gained from two studies conducted in laboratory settings. In the first (Shure, Meeker, and Hansford, 1965), pairs of bargainers shared the use of a communication device which could be used alternately (cooperation), entirely by one party (dominance), or by neither through mutual interference (standoff). In addition, each party had the power to force the other out of the device and to prevent him from using it. Finally, each party had the opportunity to give an electric shock to the other if, for example, he became irritated at the other's continued action of forcing him out of the device.

Each party in the bargaining pairs was programmed by directions and social support to act either as a pacifist or as an aggressor. The typical pacifist would (1) let the other party go first in a series of messages requiring the use of the communication device, (2) claim that alternation was fair and would seek no more time to use the device than was his fair share, (3) place his message in the device when it was his turn (with the result that his message was repeatedly forced out of the device by the aggressor), (4) not make use of any opportunity to shock the aggressor.

Given the compliant behavior of the pacifist, one might expect the aggressor eventually to feel guilty about his exploitation of the other and to adopt a more cooperative approach himself. However, when 143 aggressor-pacifist pairs interacted for 15 turns, the trend was toward greater domination of the pacifists. Only 18 of the potential aggressors

refused to use the shock from the outset. Of the remaining 125 domi-
nators, only 40 adopted a cooperative pattern by the end of the experiment, and 85 continued to dominate and to give electric shocks to the
pacifists. In general, the pacifists changed their strategy very little and
suffered continued losses to the aggressors.

The pacifist strategy was effective in causing an aggressor to cooperate only if both operators had an opportunity to send each other
messages and both used that opportunity. In such cases, the pacifist
would emphasize his desire to cooperate, would state his refusal to
shock, and would indicate his intention to suffer the shocks if the aggressor continued to act unfairly. After responding to the pacifist, the
aggressor would begin to adopt a more cooperative stance. Simply knowing, however, that the pacifist would take a cooperative approach had
no effect on the behavior of the aggressor.

Thus, it would seem that a consistent willingness to cooperate
and a refusal to exercise sanctions may simply provide the aggressor
with an opportunity to dominate the pacifist with impunity. Pacifist
tactics may even invite exploitation and aggression from some who do
not start with such intentions!

A second set of experiments shed further light on this issue
(Rapoport, 1966). These experiments involved a series of joint decisions
by two people playing a game in which the motives of each party are
mixed, that is, there are both reasons to cooperate and reasons to compete. The game is a variety of one known as the Prisoner's Dilemma
(see appendix). For example, it could occur in two firms competing for
the same market. If each firm has a choice of selling its product at a
high or a low price, both selling at a high price permits a shared market
and large profits. Similarly, both selling at a low price permits sharing.
But if one firm sells low while the other sells high, the former gains
the market and the latter either goes out of business or attempts to meet
his competitor's low price; in which case a price war ensues, and both
are unable to meet cost and to make a profit. Assuming that agreement
to sell at a high price is not possible, the most favorable outcome is to
cooperate and to share the market. In Rapoport's study, the controlled
party was directed in one instance to always cooperate, in another instance to always defect, and in a third instance to do what the opponent
did on the preceding play. As might be expected, a completely non-
cooperative strategy elicited almost no cooperation from the other party.
On the other hand, a completely cooperative strategy elicited either
complete cooperation of or complete exploitation by the other party.
The greatest amount of cooperation (70 to 80 percent) was elicited by

those who gave back what they had received on the preceding play. Apparently, cooperation is more likely to take place when each party believes that the other has the ability to compete, but instead chooses to cooperate.

Both experimental studies indicate that while cooperation based upon moral values—pacifism, helping, or avoiding the exploitation of others—may occur, the more important ingredient for inducing cooperative behavior is rational self-interest. Having both the power to retaliate and the willingness to use that power may be necessary to impress upon an opponent the cost of competition.

BELIEF SYSTEMS AND BEHAVIOR

The link between belief systems and behavior is demonstrated in the attempts we make to maintain consistency between our internal thoughts and our external behavior. So strong is this need for consistency that when beliefs and behavior differ, we will either change our belief systems to parallel our behavior or change our behavior so that it is consonant with our belief systems. For example, when an employee begins reporting to a supervisor whom he previously had not considered to be a legitimate source of influence, the employee will either increase his estimation of the supervisor's value or remove himself from the supervisor's influence. Psychotherapeutic methods operate on the same premise—that an individual cannot change to a more functional method of operation unless both his belief system and his external behavior change in a congruent manner. Introspective therapy typically attempts to change the belief system of the client, but not without also trying to guide the patient in the application of these insights so as to effect changes in external behavior. Alternately, other therapeutic methods focus on gaining successful changes in behavior, but not without also attempting to help the client internalize this new behavior into his belief system.

In this chapter we have been primarily concerned with illustrating the belief system required for the operation of problem-solving and consensus methods; we have only mentioned incidentally how these new attitudes are acquired. In Chapter 9 we shall specifically focus on the change process. We do not mean to suggest that the two topics can be entirely separated, only that each merits special attention.

NOTE ON EXPERIENTIAL LEARNING

Exercise 6 in the Appendix, "The Prisoner's Dilemma: An Exercise in Conflict and/or Cooperation," demonstrates the effect of attitudes on problem-solving or conflict behavior.

REFERENCES

Maier, N. R. *Problem Solving and Creativity in Individuals and Groups*. Brooks-Cole, 1970.

Rapoport, A. "Experiments in dyadic conflict and cooperation." *Bulletin of the Menninger Clinic* 30 (1966): 284–91.

Rogers, C. R. *On Becoming a Person*. Houghton Mifflin, 1961.

Shaw, M. E. *Group Dynamics: The Psychology of Small Group Behavior*. McGraw-Hill, 1971.

Shure, G. H., R. J. Meeker, and E. A. Hansford. "The effectiveness of pacifist strategies in bargaining games." *The Journal of Conflict Resolution* 9 (1965): 107–17.

Zand, D. E. "Trust and managerial problem solving." *Administrative Science Quarterly* 17 (1972): 229–39.

Organizing
for Conflict
or Cooperation

6

The previous chapter discussed attitudes and beliefs as they affect the tendency to engage in conflict or cooperation. In this chapter we shall focus on the organizational factors which affect these relationships. As Robert Blake says, "We organize for conflict." That is, there are planned and unplanned characteristics in both work and nonwork situations which increase the likelihood of competition or conflict. Our purpose now is to discuss ways to organize such relationships to increase the likelihood of cooperation and integrative decision making.

LEADERSHIP ROLES

Leadership in a group may reside in a single individual or may be shared among some or all members. In either case, it combines two important kinds of influence.

Process and content elements

The first kind of influence we shall call *process leadership*; it refers to the *way* that group members interact with each other or with others outside the group. For example, whether or not group members interrupt each other during group discussion is a process issue. The second kind of influence, *content leadership,* has to do with the *substance* of the influence which leaders exercise. The substance may be factual and logical, for example, having to do with giving information which applies to a problem; or it may be emotional, for example, an indication of not trusting another party.

The relative use of process and content leadership seems to vary in conflictive and cooperative situations. In bargaining, for example, the content is already largely formulated by each group or individual, and each party may distort such information while releasing it. That is, the kind of information and the extent to which it is given to the other party is an element of bargaining strategy. Intergroup communication in such situations involves voting, trading, and ranking in an attempt to arrive at a solution. Information is hoarded and exchanged for instrumental reasons, and yielding takes place as time and conditions warrant. Thus, leaders will control the process of releasing the content of information necessary to arrive at a solution.

In cooperative strategies, on the other hand, the content and process elements are more separate. Often, process leadership will be assigned to one individual who is concerned with how people are working together rather than with the content of their discussion. For example, in integrative decision making (IDM) it is important that the parties progress from a joint definition of the problem or goals to a consideration of alternatives and then to an evaluation of alternatives in three separate steps.

Many conflicts may grow out of arguments about the relative merits of two obvious solutions; the parties involved do not create a new alternative that would satisfy the needs of both. When this happens, it is also common for the focus of the discussion to be broadened from a specific disagreement to a generalized hostility.

Consider the following incident: The president of an electronics company employing 350 people had an open office which was shared with ten other people. All eleven people made a practice of getting coffee from an urn located in the corner of the room and carrying it back to their desks to drink while they worked. The company prospered and the previously tiled floor was covered with an expensive carpet. The president issued an order that no more coffee was to be drunk at the desk. Following this, two of the office members approached him, asking him to change the order. The conversation centered around arguments for and against coffee at the desk; that is, about two solutions. Gradually, the discussion escalated to hidden threats about who owned the company and about years of loyal service. A consultant who happened to be present suggested that the three people try a different approach. First, he asked the president what he wanted to achieve by forbidding coffee. He said that he did not want coffee stains on the new rug. Then the consultant asked the two employees what they wanted by having coffee, and they replied that they wanted to drink coffee at their desks. The two goals, having coffee at the desk while at the same time not staining the new rug, were written on a flip chart to direct attention *to the problem* and away from each of the parties involved.

The three people were then asked what solutions might settle the problem. They suggested such things as having someone serve coffee at the desks, covering the rug with plastic sheets, and having each employee bring his own thermos of coffee. When individuals interjected comments about the relative advantages or disadvantages of a particular alternative, the process controller (the consultant) would ask them to wait until all ideas were generated before evaluating them. After final evaluation, the parties decided to buy eleven small thermos canisters which individuals could fill at the urn and carry to their desks. Because the process controller was able to guide the parties through each of the three steps, they were able to focus attention on the problem, not on each other, and to agree on a solution that was acceptable to all.

Assigning the leadership roles

Process and content leadership often take quite different forms, and it may be advisable to separate responsibility for each in problem-solving groups. Process leadership is frequently forceful and directive, keeping the group on track as it moves through various stages of the problem-solving process. When the person chairing the meeting does not have personal objectives which must be considered in arriving at a solution, then that person may be the process controller and avoid involvement in the content discussion. On the other hand, when the chairperson does have vested interests, it is best to appoint another person to act as process controller.

Furthermore, problem-solving groups can increase their effectiveness by separating the process elements of their interactions from content considerations. This may be done by reserving a period at the end of the meeting to review how the group interacted and processed information. Observers or process controllers can give feedback to the group or its individuals, and group members can discuss their own process issues.

Content leadership, unlike process leadership, does not tend to be focused or directive. When relatively small groups are involved, all parties participate equally and leadership will rotate among members as issues change or discussion develops. When large groups are involved (particularly where there are two large factions), interaction may be limited to representatives of the larger group or groups. In such cases it is important that group members *instruct* their leaders about their needs and about possible solutions which they find acceptable.

The instruction of the content leader by group members will avoid placing the leader "up front." For example, when a group fails to instruct its leader and merely places him or her in a representative position, the group will often take credit for his or her successes. It will also criticize or reject the leader should the group's desires not be achieved. It becomes the leader's fault if outcomes are not satisfactory. On the other hand, when a group instructs its leaders about needs and outcomes, the group shares responsibility for the leadership process. Should outcomes not prove satisfactory, the group is more likely to say "we failed" instead of "our leader failed."

ORGANIZING TO AVOID CONFLICT

When a single group is split into opposing competitive or con-flictive factions, group members generally believe it to be in their interest to present a united front to the other party regardless of how much they disagree among themselves. They feel that to disagree in front of the opposing group would decrease the likelihood of their winning. Yet, there is evidence that disagreement within groups in the presence of potential opponents, called *dissensus,* has positive value. There is also evidence that such behavior by one side and not the other is not necessarily disadvantageous (Druckman, 1968).

The desirability of a joint agenda

Ideally, organizing to avoid conflict suggests that groups should meet together to develop a joint agenda of problems to be discussed rather than meeting separately to prepare separate agenda. In joint meetings, members of both groups indicate that problems of one group are worth serious attention by the other, and that successful problem solving will take place only if all group members attack the problems together.

More often, however, groups will have already developed an opposing stance. Experimental evidence from simulated labor-management bargaining situations provides a clue on how to progress from such a state.

Positive value of dissensus

Evan and MacDougall (1967) created three combinations of negotiating teams: (1) teams representing a unified front (that is, a pairing of equally extreme bargainers) on both labor and management sides; (2) a disagreeing pair (one moderate and one extreme bargainer) on both sides; and (3) a unified pair on one side and a disagreeing pair on the other. The investigators then sought to determine the effect of these alignments in five negotiating sessions in achieving integrating, compromising, or dominating behavior.

Their results indicate that (1) bilateral dissensus—open disagreement on both sides in the presence of each other—produced more agreement than bilateral unity or unilateral dissensus; (2) bilateral dissensus produced more integrative behavior than unilateral dissensus; (3) it was not clear whether more integrative behavior was produced with bilateral dissensus than with unilateral unity; and (4) there was no evidence that unilateral dissensus led to more domination by the group displaying a unified front. Although experimental, these conclusions are not inconsistent with other evidence. Field studies of real groups which arrive at consensus rather than splitting into conflict indicate that consensus is more likely to develop when stated member needs, whether the substance is factual or emotional, are met in the course of meetings (Guetzkow and Gyr, 1954). Apparently, suppressing one's wishes in order to provide a unified front to the opposition may actually hinder the achievement of integrative group decisions.

Techniques to dispel open warfare

Another situation in intergroup relations is one in which open warfare has broken out, and it becomes necessary to break the cycle of win-lose relations and to substitute the belief that agreement is possible. Blake and Mouton (1962) have described various approaches which have been used in four union-management warfare situations to reestablish a collaborative relationship:

Training in the theory and behavior of conflict resolution • Members of hostile groups may participate in a common laboratory learning situation (variously known as laboratory training, T-groups, or sensitivity training) in which they experience the consequences of win-lose and win-win behavior and gain the theoretical perspective surrounding these methods. Thus, in a controlled setting opposing group members are able to gain valid experience about the costs of win-lose methods and to practice alternative behavior.

Norm-setting conferences • Essentially this approach entails a shift from control by a single individual to group sharing of responsibility. Group members using this approach consolidate their ideas about future action by discussing the attitudes, reservations, doubts, and hopes of each of them concerning cooperation with a former adversary, and by establishing rules of group behavior. Thus, group members commit themselves to standards of behavior which will lead to win-win relations.

Behavioral science intervention • This approach entails intervention during group interaction to head off damaging consequences of conflictive behavior. In such cases, a process controller will freeze a situation long enough to focus attention on behavior and to indicate the likely consequences of such behavior. Even if group members have theoretical and practical experience with integrative methods, it is easy for them to fall back into old methods of behavior in the heat of an argument. By stopping the activity and calling attention to process issues, the leader may maintain the group's orientation to collaborative methods. An example of such an approach occurred recently when the author was observing a group make a series of judgmental decisions. Two members disagreed on an issue and suddenly one member said to the other, "Damn it, use your head. You are being inconsistent. You said one thing a minute ago and now you are saying another." The author stopped the interaction and asked the accused party how he felt about what was said. The accused reported that he was angry and that he was *not* being inconsistent. The interventionist then asked the accuser how he could change his original statement from a judgmental accusation to a description. The accuser then asked the other member, "Why did you change your description of the situation on this problem when you said something different on the problem which we discussed earlier?" The accused member responded that he had more facts now and realized that his earlier statement had been wrong. The accuser then said, "I guess I really prevented you from changing, didn't I?"

Leveling conferences • Reminiscent of the dissensus issue, Blake and Mouton's final approach is to ask members of "warring" groups to meet together to explore their attitudes, feelings, and previous behavior. They may review their history of interaction and consider alternatives to win-lose activity. Sometimes a description of one party's perceptions of itself as well as of the other party will be effective. For example, the members of each group may be asked to describe how they view the other group and how they describe themselves; then both groups may meet to compare their descriptions. Often such an activity will bring out the self-fulfilling prophecies, the stereotypes, and the misinterpretations of behavior and motivation that obstruct effective problem solving. Blake and Mouton suggest that such conferences be channeled through representatives of each group with the other members present but silent in order to promote more orderly flow of communication. Yet, the author's experience suggests that such strict channeling of response need not be followed, and that more open communication may take place when all members interact together as well.

SPACE AS A FACTOR IN CONFLICT RESOLUTION

A few years ago the author was preparing to do a survey of joint apprentice committees and visited several such committees to observe their operations. Joint apprenticeship committees administer entrance into apprenticeship programs and monitor the progress of apprentices through their educational and training program. Such committees are composed of both employer and union representatives. One of the committees visited met in a dining hall of a local vocational school. By chance, there were several substitute members on both the employer and the union sides, and visitors from the state and federal apprenticeship services also were present. When the group assembled, the identity of the union, employer, and visitor members was not immediately clear. At the beginning of the meeting the arrangement was that shown in Figure 6–1(A). By the end of the meeting, the positions of the members and visitors had altered to that shown in Figure 6–1(B): The adversaries had physically grouped themselves into a clear we-they arrangement, with the neutral parties (the visitors) looking on from a detached position. Since a we-they distinction is a necessary element of conflict, the participants had organized themselves in a manner that could promote such conflict.

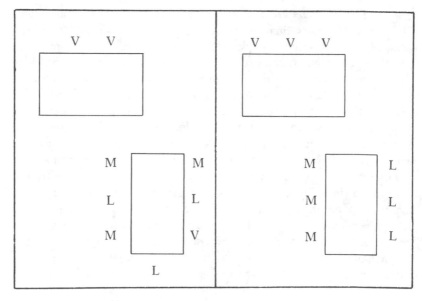

A) At the Start   B) At the Finish

FIGURE 6–1.   Spatial Arrangements of Labor (L), Management (M), and Visitors (V) at Joint Apprentice Committee Meeting.

Spatial arrangement as nonverbal language

The preceding example should suggest that, in part, spatial arrangements are defined according to expectations about the behavior of others. In addition, spatial arrangements will themselves provoke or elicit various forms of behavior. Once committee members learned the identity of one another, they moved to different locations around the tables. Perhaps they were more comfortable in the new positions; or, perhaps, they moved to the places where they felt that they were supposed to be. Whatever the reason, the committee members changed their positions without conscious choice; and their new positions might well elicit new forms of interaction. In their new locations the labor and management representatives had "faced off" across the table. It should be pointed out that the observers were physically detached from the confrontation.

Spatial arrangements influence relations in various ways. The relative positions of group members can determine who will be selected or accepted as leader. For example, a person sitting at the end of a rectangular table is likely to be a previously determined leader or is more likely to be selected as the leader. In a study of simulated jury deliberations, the foreman was seated at the head of the table, participated in the discussion more than the other jurors, and was considered to have made the most significant contributions by the other members of the group (Strodtbeck and Hook, 1961). It appears that favored positions are often self-selected by those in power, but also that those in such positions are more likely to be accepted as leaders as well.

When two parties are seated on one side of a table and three on the other, more often than not the two-party side will contain the person identified as the leader (Howells and Becker, 1962). Thus, to equalize power and distribute leadership among members of a group, it is appropriate to provide undifferentiated locations for all group members. It may be useful to use a circular arrangement for a group and to insure that subgroups of members are not clustered together.

The nonverbal signals of distance between parties also create attitudes which may affect problem-solving behavior. For example, in analyzing the effects of distance on perception of others in a group, it was found that the more distance there was between persons, the less friendly, acquainted, and talkative each perceived the other to be (Russo, 1967). Which is cause and which is effect is not clear. People who feel cool toward each other may take distant positions; on the other hand, people in distant positions may feel cool toward each other. In fact, both probably occur; in either case distance clearly affects interaction.

Proprietary uses of space

The significance of the preceding examples is suggested by the information currently available about how people use space. Three concepts are relevant: group territory, individual territory, and personal space. The first two refer to fixed areas over which a group or an individual takes a proprietary interest. Personal space, on the other hand, has to do with the self-established area of privacy and control which surrounds a person. Of the three, our immediate concern shall be with the implications of group and individual territoriality.

Groups may establish boundaries around territory which they seek to protect against intruders. Certain street-corner gangs and ethnic groups define their territory and defend it with violence. The author recalls a situation in which two laboratory training groups were meeting in separate rooms at the same resort. When a member of one group entered the room of the other, he was lifted physically and carried out. In a business organization, the members of one department may tease a member of another department who has entered their territory.

Employees in a company may naturally divide into groups according to the location of their work space—those in the front office versus those in the plant, or those upstairs versus those on the main floor; and such group identifications may contribute to eventual conflict between the groups.

In one company known to the author, the potential conflict and divisiveness of space has been reduced by minimizing physical boundaries, by requiring a sharing of territory, and by providing common problem-solving rooms for everyone's use. The firm has avoided the use of walls and private offices. Instead, desks are grouped in large rooms containing a variety of activities. A potential division between engineering and manufacturing has been minimized by having engineers and production people work together at the production line, running prototypes through the regular production facilities. When problems do occur, those people who can contribute solutions move to one of several meeting rooms. The rooms are common territory and are provided with flip charts and blackboards. The latter focus attention on the problem and, furthermore, minimize the split into factions or subgroups.

Like group territory, individual territory is a proprietary claim of space which an individual makes for his own use. Thus, a person may lay claim to a particular chair, a bed, a workbench. A primitive example of this tendency to define individual territory was dramatically illustrated by a woman attending a sensitivity training session in New England. One afternoon she found a meadow which she claimed as her own. She paced off the boundaries of her territory, urinated on the ground, removed her clothes, and lay in the grass. Anyone approaching the spatial boundaries was directed to leave—it was *her* space.

While such dramatic means are not used to define space in business organizations, the tendency to own a location exists, nevertheless. Such space apparently provides a means for establishing security and predictability. When Party A is invited into Party B's office to discuss a problem, A is less secure than B, and A's problem-solving capabilities may be diminished as a result of anxiety. For this reason, the use of neutral territory for problem solving may be more desirable.

*"Gentlemen, instead of trying to mediate this thing, why
don't you just slug it out?"*
Reprinted by permission of the publisher from *Personnel*, May/June 1968,
© 1968 by the American Management Association, Inc.

Territoriality and styles of conflict resolution

The relationship between space and styles of conflict resolution
is suggested in a series of studies by Sommer (1969). Given the seating
arrangements shown in Figure 6–2, people chose corner-to-corner
or face-to-face arrangements for casual conversation, side-by-side arrangements for cooperation, distant patterns for co-action, and face-to-face
arrangements for competition. This and other studies indicate that, in
general, people seem to prefer a side-by-side arrangement for cooperation
and a face-to-face arrangement for competition. It is not clear whether
the positions help to elicit cooperation or conflict or whether they are
merely chosen on the basis of such feelings. There is evidence, however,
that people seated in a formal arrangement will score higher on a scale
designed to measure anxiety elicited by the situation than people in an
informal seating arrangement (Myers, 1969). Whether some positions
are more rewarding than others or certain positions create expectations
about potential interaction, the unspoken language of spatial positions

FIGURE 6–2.   Seating Preferences at Rectangular Tables. Robert Sommer, *Personal Space: The Behavioral Basis of Design* © 1969. Reprinted by permission of Prentice-Hall, Inc., Englewood Cliffs, New Jersey.

Seating Arrangement	Percentage of Students Choosing This Arrangement			
	Condition 1 (Conversing)	Condition 2 (Cooperating)	Condition 3 (Coacting)	Condition 4 (Competing)
X on top-left side	42	19	3	7
X on both left and right sides	46	25	32	41
X top-left and bottom-right	1	5	43	20
X top-left and bottom-center	0	0	3	5
X top-left and bottom-left	11	51	7	8
X top-center and bottom-center	0	0	13	18
Total	100	100	100	99

does seem to influence the potential cooperative and competitive relationship of people.

The relationship between individual and group space may be observed in a group which meets together over an extended time period. Initially, group members will seek the security of their own individual space, returning again and again to the same place at the table, the same chair, or merely the same place on the floor. Group territory is only vaguely defined. However, as the group becomes more cohesive and group members begin collectively to take responsibility for the group, the group territory will become clearly identified and group members will move about the room with ease, seating themselves in different locations. Process leaders may want to encourage such a development by suggesting that group members take different positions in a series of meetings.

Personal space needs

The third concept of spatial arrangement is that of personal space. Unlike territoriality, which is fixed, personal space is relative to one's own body and moves with the individual. Its limits also are flexible, for it is associated with how the individual feels about others—intimate, personal, impersonal—and it extends to the point at which a person is no longer comfortable when approached by another. Awareness of personal space requirements is useful for those interested in avoiding conflict, since a violation of personal space elicits negative reactions.

Obviously, at any given time such factors as personality, the environment, perception of the role of another, and purpose of the interaction determine an individual's personal space needs. On this basis, Edward Hall (1968) has categorized personal space in terms of four zones: the intimate, the personal, the social, and the public zones. He has estimated that, in general, the intimate zone for Americans is from the surface of the skin to 18 inches. That is, we seem to have an invisible bubble around us and into which we allow others to enter only under special circumstances. It is the intimate zone that is used for lovemaking, comforting, and protecting. Where it becomes necessary to enter the intimate zone for other purposes, the purpose must be clear and understood. Thus, the physician or dentist is permitted to do so only according to strictly defined role prescriptions. In other cases, as in a crowded elevator or subway, the person entering the intimate zone is objectified, and viewed as an object rather than as a person.

Hall's second zone is the personal zone, ranging from 1½ to 4 feet around a person. This range is used for comfortable interaction with others and connotes closeness and friendship. The third zone, the social, is from 4 to 12 feet from the person. At the closer end of this third zone we conduct most impersonal business. People working together will maintain such spacing. The outer edge connotes more formal interactions, where people are more insulated from each other. Finally, the public zone of more than 12 feet represents distancing beyond the range of comfortable interaction. Hall mentions that public figures will frequently keep a public zone of 30 feet around themselves. That distance is mentioned in White's description of the night the Democrats nominated John F. Kennedy as their presidential candidate (1961, p. 171):

> Kennedy loped into the cottage with his light, dancing step, as young and lithe as springtime, and called a greeting to those who stood in his way. Then he seemed to slip from them as he descended the steps of the split-level cottage to a corner where his brother Bobby and brother-in-law Sargent Shriver were chatting, waiting for him. The others in the room surged forward on impulse to join him. Then they halted. *A distance of perhaps thirty feet separated them from him, but it was impassable.* [My italics] They stood apart, these men of long-established power, and watched him. He turned after a few minutes, saw them watching him, and whispered to his brother-in-law. Shriver now crossed the separating space to invite them over. First Averell Harriman; then Dick Daley; then Mike DiSalle; then, one by one, in an order determined by the candidate's own instinct and judgment, he let them all congratulate him. Yet no one could pass the little open distance between him and them uninvited, because they were there not as his patrons but as his clients. They could come by invitation only, for this might be a President of the United States.

Research findings about personal space

Propositions regarding personal space based on controlled studies have been summarized by Shaw (1971):

1) Personal space contracts in the presence of impersonal objects and expands in relation to more personal objects. For example, in one study (Little, 1965, pp. 237–47) subjects were asked to arrange figures on various background settings: a living room, an office, and a street corner. It was expected that the interfigure distance would increase as the space became more impersonal. In fact, women conformed to this prediction but men, interestingly enough, did not. In another study (McBride, King, and James, 1965, pp. 153–57) subjects showed a greater reaction, as measured by galvanic skin response, when touched by another person than when touched by an inanimate object.

2) People establish a characteristic distance between themselves and others but this varies according to the setting of the interaction and the relationship between the parties. For example, a study by Willis (1966, pp. 221–22) indicated that persons of the same age interact more closely with each other than do people of different ages, and acquaintances interact more closely than strangers.

3) Individuals devise various techniques to guard against invasion. For example, Sommer (1969) conducted a number of investigations in which subjects reacted to the invasion of their personal space by exhibiting feelings of discomfort and defensive gestures. If these defensive reactions failed to inhibit intruders, subjects most frequently departed rather than accept the situation.

Keeping in mind our strictures relating to leadership and space and the techniques for avoiding open warfare, we shall proceed in Chapter 7 to a discussion of the relational conditions, perceptions, and attitudes necessary for the successful operation of integrative decision making.

REFERENCES

Blake, R. R., and J. S. Mouton. "Comprehension of own and outgroup positions under intergroup competition." *Sociometry* 24 (1961a): 177–83.
Blake, R. R., and J. S. Mouton. "The intergroup dynamics of win-lose conflict and problem-solving collaboration in union-manage-

ment relations." In *Intergroup Relations and Leadership,* M. Sherif, ed., pp. 94–140. Wiley, 1962.

Druckman, D. "Prenegotiation experience and dyadic conflict resolution in a bargaining situation." *Journal of Experimental Social Psychology* 4 (1968): 367–83.

Evan, W. M., and J. A. MacDougall. "Interorganizational conflict: A labor-management bargaining experiment." *Journal of Conflict Resolution* 11 (1967): 398–413.

Guetzkow, H., and J. Gyr. "An analysis of conflict in decision-making groups." *Human Relations* 7 (1954): 367–81.

Hall, E. T. *The Hidden Dimension.* Doubleday, 1968.

Howells, L. T., and S. W. Becker. "Seating arrangement and leadership emergence." *Journal of Abnormal and Social Psychology* 64 (1962): 148–50.

Little, K. B. "Personal space." *Journal of Experimental Social Psychology* 1 (1965): 237–47.

McBride, G., M. G. King, and J. W. James. "Social proximity effects on GSR in adult humans." *Journal of Psychology* 61 (1965): 153–57.

Myers, R. K. "Some effects of seating arrangements in counseling." Unpublished doctoral dissertation, University of Florida, 1969.

Russo, N. F. "Connotation of seating arrangements." *Cornell Journal of Social Relations* 2 (1967): 37–44.

Shaw, M. E. *Group Dynamics: The Psychology of Small Group Behavior.* McGraw-Hill, 1971.

Sommer, R. *Personal Space: The Behavioral Basis of Design.* Prentice-Hall, 1969.

Strodtbeck, F. L., and L. H. Hook. "The social dimensions of a twelve-man jury table." *Sociometry* 24 (1961): 397–415.

White, T. H. *The Making of the President 1960.* Atheneum, 1961.

Willis, F. N., Jr. "Initial speaking distance as a function of the speaker's relationship." *Psychonomic Science* 5 (1966): 221–22.

Early Stages of Integrative Decision Making

7

In the second chapter we outlined the factors contributing to overt conflict and the consequent need to resolve the conflict once it has developed. We then considered the various forms of conflict resolution and the way in which language, personal styles, attitudes, and situational conditions contribute to conflict or problem solving. We now summarize the processes and conditions associated with forcing (win-lose), compromising (lose-lose), and problem-solving (win-win) methods. Then we turn to the integrative decision-making method (IDM) itself, specifically to its initial stages. It should be apparent at this point that problem solving is the opposite of conflict. That is, one has a choice between engaging in behavior which defeats one or both parties or behavior which provides a mutually satisfactory solution to a problem.

FORCING

Problem-solving methods are quite different both from methods in which one party attempts to force the other to comply and from methods which attempt to find a compromise between parties. In forcing, both parties assume that the gain of one party necessitates the other's loss, and therefore each seeks to defeat the other so that all gain is on one side. Forcing entails the imposition of goals, methods, rules, and values. Strategic considerations prior to conflict are aimed at defeating the opponent; since resources are viewed as fixed and limited, each party is anxious to obtain the maximum share.

Forcing depends upon real or perceived power imbalances between the parties. Each will attempt to maximize relative ability to reward or to punish the other through control of information, money, formal authority, desired associations, and the like (Filley and House, 1969). Energies of the parties are directed against each other rather than against a common problem, and the content of the conflict becomes generalized from a specific issue to an atmosphere of bitter dispute. Offensive and defensive strategies replace facts and reason, and each party attempts to present a strong united front to the other. Forcing strategies lead the parties to assume fixed positions to emphasize the most obvious or accessible solution rather than actually defining the problem, and to communicate with each other in a judgmental and accusatory, rather than a factual, manner.

Furthermore, differences rather than similarities are emphasized; those similarities that do exist are actually denied. Each party will distort the image of the other to justify its own right to conquest. Thus, the controlling group will characterize the controlled as uninformed, weak, childlike, or dependent. The needs, feelings, and attitudes of the opposition are ignored to avoid identification with their position. Leaders in warring factions are selected on the basis of their ability to force the opponent to capitulate, rather than on the basis of skills in social facilitation, and each party will arrange itself hierarchically for aggressive purposes. Both between and within warring factions, feedback is limited to reports of accomplishment or capitulation, rather than conveying mutually beneficial information. The forcing strategy ends when (1) one party capitulates or manifests no further overt opposition or (2) a deadlock occurs.

COMPROMISING

Compromising methods are similar to forcing in the assumption of limited resources and in the resultant conflict of interests. They differ, however, in the assumption that both parties will arrive at a sharing of fixed resources and in the assumption of a relatively equal balance of power between the parties. That is, total capitulation by either party is viewed as disadvantageous by the other. The parties are interdependent and continued disagreement is seen as more costly than compromise.

Strategic considerations in compromising are aimed at effecting a favored outcome. Each party attempts to increase his relative power, and particular emphasis is placed upon the strategic use of information. Bargaining strategies are defined, opponent strategies anticipated, and problems and issues are posed in terms of strategic value rather than in terms of any real priority. Information is hoarded or distorted to provide relative advantage in negotiations and exchanged for manipulative reasons. Like forcing, compromising directs the energies of the parties toward each other, rather than toward a solution to a common problem. Substantive issues are approached as solutions rather than defined as problems.

Parties involved in compromise are concerned with sacrificing and with avoiding an unfavorable share of the outcome, rather than with achieving a solution beneficial to both parties. For example, Maier makes an analogy between a compromise strategy and two parties fighting over an orange. The parties eventually compromise and cut the orange in half, yet accurate communication of needs may have indicated that one party wanted the orange for juice while the other wanted the orange peel to make candy (1973, p. 629).

As in forcing, groups employing compromising strategies become hierarchically arranged and present a united front to the opponent. Communication within a group is directed to the chief negotiator and communication between groups occurs through leadership for both sides. Negotiators, concerned about saving face with their constituents, will manipulate both the subjective and objective aspects of the negotiation with feigned anger or frustration in an attempt to elicit an advantageous response from the opposing party. Emotional conflict is avoided, however, since it might make the situation uncontrollable.

As in forcing, the image of the opposing party in compromising is distorted; opponents are stereotyped and statements made to the other party are often accusatory and judgmental. Compromising ends when both parties agree to accept the decision. Such agreements are often accompanied by arrangements for future reciprocity, and neither party is entirely satisfied with the outcome.

PROBLEM SOLVING

In contrast with parties engaged in forcing and compromising, parties engaged in problem solving assume that it is possible to arrive at a solution which is of high quality and which is mutually acceptable. The parties see resources as abundant and have like interests in finding an acceptable solution. The energies of the parties are directed toward defeating the problem.

The content of problem-solving discussions is maintained at a specific, descriptive level of interaction. Both facts and personal feelings are reported, and feedback is given to others without accusation or judgment. Areas of agreement and disagreement are clarified. Since trust levels are high, parties permit mutual influence through open reporting of facts and feelings; every attempt is made to ensure that all information is shared. Particular attention is placed upon clarifying the problem and upon ensuring that all alternatives are considered before selection of one takes place.

Parties in problem-solving discussions interact freely with each other in a nonhierarchical pattern. Process control may be vested in one member, but content leadership will change freely as different issues are discussed. Dominating and yielding behavior as well as mechanisms which avoid confronting the facts (voting, trading, resort to rules) are avoided. The typical outcome of problem solving is a high-quality solution to which both parties are committed.

ELEMENTS IN THE IDM PROCESS

An understanding of forcing, compromising, and problem-solving methods is a necessary ingredient in developing skills associated with integrative decision making. Yet such an understanding is only the first step. The next step is learning each of the stages in the integrative decision-making process. The stages in IDM have been implicitly described in earlier chapters; they may now be identified explicitly:

1) *Review and adjustment of relational conditions*—the comparison of the objective conditions in which the parties are

related with conditions known to promote cooperation rather than conflict and the possible adjustment of those conditions.

2) *Review and adjustment of perceptions*—the use of reality testing to determine facts regarding the parties.

3) *Review and adjustment of attitudes*—the use of reality testing of feelings and attitudes between the parties.

4) *Problem definition*—the mutual determination of the depersonalized problem.

5) *Search for solutions*—the nonjudgmental generation of possible solutions to the problem.

6) *Consensus decision*—the evaluation of alternative solutions and the agreement on a single solution.

The first three elements of the IDM process—review and adjustment of relational conditions, review and adjustment of perceptions, and review and adjustment of attitudes—will be specifically discussed in this chapter; problem definition, search for solutions, and consensus decision, however, will be taken up in Chapter 8.

The elements of IDM are depicted in Figure 7–1. As indicated, the review and adjustment of relational conditions, individual perceptions, and individual attitudes are interrelated and not entirely separable. For example, reality testing of attitudes may result in an adjustment of attitudes, which in turn may lead to changed perceptions and a consequent adjustment of relational conditions. For purposes of exposition, however, we shall have to separate them. As further indicated in Figure 7–1, the steps in the integrative process are permeated with perceptions and attitudes. If the parties have difficulty in achieving a mutual problem definition or a joint determination of alternative solutions, it may be necessary to return to a review and adjustment of perceptions or attitudes before progressing further.

A central concept in these early stages is that of *reality testing*. Since we see the world through the emotional screens of individual perceptions and attitudes, it is often necessary to determine the extent to which the screens exist and the extent to which perceptions match reality.

Similarly, when two parties perceive a situation in which the gain of one party must be at the other's expense, they may find that their perceptions are correct in fact; and in such cases it may not be possible to restructure the relationship so that it is nonconflictive. On

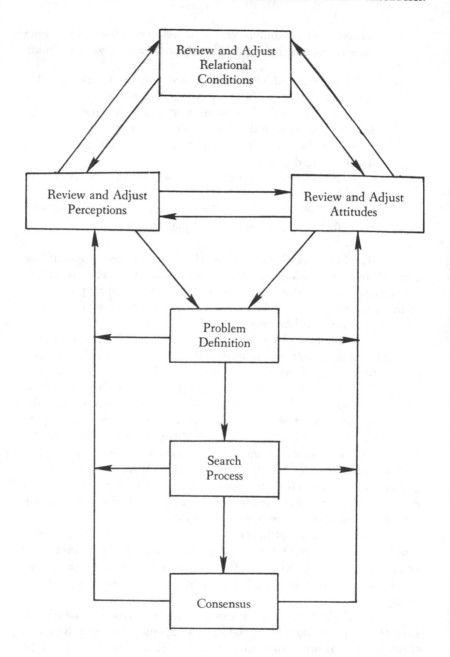

FIGURE 7–1.   The Integrative Decision-Making Method

the other hand, it may be true that such perceptions of the situation are not correct but are based upon a limited search for solutions, in which case alternative solutions should be formulated.

Conditions existing between the parties, reasoning processes, and emotions are givens which should objectively be studied by both parties for their mutual benefit, without making any judgments about their worth.

REVIEW AND ADJUSTMENT OF RELATIONAL CONDITIONS

In Chapter 1 we discussed a number of conditions which are frequently antecedent to conflict. After such conditions are identified, it may be possible to adjust them in a manner which promotes cooperation or avoids the likelihood of conflict. For example, boundary conditions which are ambiguous may be clarified. In this sense, the question parties ask each other becomes, "How can we clarify the jurisdictions which are ambiguous in a manner which we both find acceptable and appropriate?" The situation then lends itself to problem solving.

In other cases, the existence of conditions which are themselves conflictive merely creates surmountable obstacles for problem solving. For example, the Weather Bureau and NASA both have an interest in developing satellites to photograph the earth for purposes of weather prediction. Each exists as a separate agency with physically separate facilities. After a history of serious conflict the parties have developed a cooperative relationship (Delbecq and Filley, 1972). One mechanism for maintaining understanding has been what might be called "the doctrine of no surprises." Through this doctrine, each party takes great pains to ensure that an informal agreement and understanding is attained before initiating a formal action. That is, before sending a letter to the other party to initiate action, the initiating party will contact the other informally to describe the purpose and meaning of the communication and to ensure that the responding party understands and agrees with the proposed action.

Relational conditions apply to the specific environment in which potential problem solving will take place. To gain an understanding of the existing conditions and of ways to optimize their potential for problem solving, the following questions based on ideas in Chapters 6 and 7 might be asked:

1) Do the spatial arrangements promote equality and avoid divisiveness? Problem solving should take place on neutral territory with parties arranged in a nonconfrontational manner which directs attention and energy toward the problem.

2) Are time constraints minimized? Problem solving occurs most readily where the parties are not pressured by deadlines.

3) Is group size controlled to facilitate interaction and avoid divisiveness? Groups of five to seven people are most appropriate for interaction and member satisfaction. Larger groups may be used, but member interaction is reduced and restricted.

4) Is the communication process arranged so that all members communicate with each other rather than having communication channeled through a single group representative? The former arrangement will promote problem solving; and the latter, conflictive relations.

5) Is the leader of the group controlling the process of group interaction rather than its content? Process leaders make sure that the necessary steps in the problem-solving process take place, rather than promoting their own preferred solutions, as do content leaders.

6) Is information shared by all parties rather than hoarded by some to be used for their own strategic advantage? Shared information promotes trust and reduces differences of power associated with monopolies of information. Hoarded information reduces trust, creates power differences, and increases the potential for conflict.

7) Are opportunities provided to deal with problems as they occur rather than reserving them for discussion at a later date? Delays permit facts to be lost and positions distorted; problem solving is facilitated when parties can handle problems as they occur.

It may not be possible to adjust relational conditions to derive the maximum benefit for problem solving, but even so, a recognition of their favorable or unfavorable contribution to the problem-solving process will permit these conditions to be viewed as surmountable obstacles. For example, if there is to be an unavoidable delay in problem solving because of some incident, the parties can preclude a loss of facts by making efforts to record details of the incident at the time it occurs.

REVIEW AND ADJUSTMENT OF PERCEPTIONS

Individual perceptions of a situation are adjusted and corrected by reality testing. Here, each individual asks himself, "Am I viewing the situation or the behavior as it actually exists?" As a general rule, perceptions are more likely to be correct as the number of measures of the condition increases. That is, perceptions become more accurate as an individual obtains more facts about the condition and as his impressions are confirmed by the perceptions of others.

If Party A perceives that Party B is exhibiting self-oriented behavior in problem-solving situations, A can increase the likelihood that his perception is based upon reality by increasing the number of observations that he makes of B's behavior or by asking others involved whether they have observed the same behavior.

Perceptions are linked to the parties' assessment of conditions surrounding them and also to their recognition of solutions that are available. If the parties see only two solutions to a problem (my way versus your way), then the possibility of finding a mutually beneficial solution is seriously limited. As in the previous example, these perceptions should be evaluated by reality testing to determine whether other solutions do in fact exist.

Perceptions also influence the parties' assessments of each others' positions. Many inferences may be drawn from a few facts; fewer inferences are possible as the number of facts increases. Here the notions of closed-ended versus open-ended communication are helpful. *Closed ended* communication is communication that permits only yes/no or multiple-choice responses. For example, if I make a proposal to you and ask if you like it, I restrict your response to yes or no. If I say, "How do you like my proposal—do you think it is well written, that it is too long, or that it expresses an interesting idea?" then I restrict your response to one of these three choices. In contrast, *open-ended* communication means asking a question such as "What do you think of this proposal?" and then waiting for your answer without setting limits on it, leaving you free to express your thoughts about the proposal. I can then ask further questions to elicit more information. It is appropriate to recall that facts, rather than judgments and accusations, help to resolve differences by clarifying the position of another which may have been misperceived.

Finally, perceptions alter the parties' approach to problem solving. Implicit in much conflictive behavior is the notion that conflict is the only way to resolve differences. We have further stated that individuals will selectively address those conflicts for which solutions can be routinely achieved over those for which the solution is unprogrammed. In this connection, one of the functions of manifest conflict is its triggering effect in eliciting some form of resolution process, be it suppression, compromise, or problem solving. If parties understand and can use integrative methods, then these methods will be elicited when conflict occurs, and the potential for creative solutions will thereby be increased.

This creative potential is illustrated in the case of a conflict between management and labor regarding income guarantees for workers in the auto industry:

> During the 1955 automobile negotiations, the UAW vigorously pressed for some form of guaranteed annual wage. The demand was important to the union because of the need to take care of unemployed automobile workers. The specific form of the program advanced by the UAW conflicted with several of management's objectives, but eventually an accommodative and quite integrative arrangement was worked out— one that limited the company's cost liability, coordinated the Supplemental Unemployment Benefit plan with state unemployment compensation, and kept the level of benefits at a point where there was still some incentive to work. These had been the critical concerns of management. From the union's point of view, the plan went a long way toward securing the objectives of the originally proposed GAW and was regarded as an important union achievement. (Walton and McKersie, 1965, p. 135)

The conflict precipitated an integrative search for a solution which would meet the needs of both management and labor and resulted in an entirely new form of private income guarantee for industry.

REVIEW AND ADJUSTMENT OF ATTITUDES

The attitudes and feelings of individuals constitute another screen through which information about conditions or other parties is processed, sometimes distorted, and frequently judged. These attitudes and feelings must therefore be tested by the parties in an IDM relationship. Attitudes and feelings are ignored in some strategies and manipulated in others; in IDM they are dealt with directly and objectively.

Unlike the reality testing of perceptions, reality testing of attitudes has to do with the internal processes of an individual. A change in attitudes cannot be ordered or directed by someone or something external to the person. Recalling the transactional analysis model in Chapter 3, Party A cannot change Party B's fear of failing on a project by telling him that it is wrong to worry, that it is not logical to worry, or that he will succeed. A may help B's internal processing, however, by asking for the evidence that B has that suggests failure might occur, or by asking for examples of similar projects in which B was engaged and the outcome of those projects. That is, A may help B change from a subjective state of generalized fear to an objective assessment of the likelihood of failing based upon his previous experience. Such interactions are not significantly different from the contrast between judgmental or accusatory statements ("You make me angry") and factual or descriptive statements ("When you shout at me I get feelings of anger") about a certain event.

At this juncture we may also note that attitudes and feelings are themselves neither favorable nor unfavorable; only the effects of such attitudes may be judged favorably or unfavorably. Anger, desire, joy—and distaste for seafood, for that matter—are simply feelings which reside in the individual. Attitudes and feelings are givens to be identified and understood since they enter into the problem-solving relationship. It is better, by far, to make attitudes and feelings explicit than to deal with their behavioral manifestations, not knowing the origins of or the reasons for such behavior.

Insofar as possible, the attitudes and feelings of parties who will engage in IDM should be identified specifically, before the process takes place. Since integrative methods depend upon trust, mutuality, and cooperation, they have little chance of success if the parties are distrustful, hostile, and competitive. If the parties have the resources to arrive at integrative solutions but exhibit hostility toward each other, there is little chance of agreement. Where attitudes are found to be dysfunctional, attempts should be made to adjust them before problem definition begins. If a change in such attitudes is not immediately possible, the best strategy may be for the parties to separate or to deal with trivial, easily solved problems (Guetzkow and Gyr, 1954).

Attitudes and feelings always enter into the integrative process at the time of problem definition in the form of goals or values held by the parties. At that point, they are essentially accepted by the parties without any attempts to adjust them—ideally being expressed as specific preferences about needs or agenda items rather than as generalized feelings of hostility or competition.

As suggested in Chapter 5, attitudes and feelings of individuals are often related to their personality structures. One such personality characteristic, for example, is authoritarianism. The authoritarian personality exhibits conservatism, a desire to be directed or to direct, a need for rules and order, emotional coldness, and some forms of hostility toward minority groups. Persons scoring high on authoritarianism are both less trusting of others and less trustworthy in their own behavior (Haythorn, 1956). Similarly, those low an authoritarianism are less likely to act in a one-sided manner (Deutsch, 1960).

Self-esteem also is a determinant of individuals' attitudes and behavior. Various studies indicate that those low in self-esteem (1) are more likely to feel threatened in a situation, (2) are more vulnerable and dependent upon a power laden situation, (3) have greater need for structure, (4) inhibit aggression, (5) are easily persuaded, and (6) yield more to group pressure than those high in self-esteem (Janis, 1954; Kagan and Missen, 1956; Cohen, 1954).

Personality traits have an effect on potential problem solving; thus, they should be considered when selecting parties for integrative decision making. Where possible, it would be most convenient to select parties for decision making whose personalities favor integrative methods. If the selection of parties with favorable personalities is not possible, the integrative process can still be learned and applied. In such cases, however, more effort will go into working out attitudinal difficulties.

We have mentioned other attitudes throughout this book which are important to the achievement of integrative solutions. Briefly, we suggested that: (1) the needs of other parties must be felt to be legitimate and sincere; (2) the other party should be viewed as a helpful resource; (3) there must be a genuine belief that mutual benefit is preferable to the exclusive gain of one party; (4) there must be a belief that an integrative solution is possible; and (5), rather than second-guessing the motives, attitudes, and feelings of others, it is better to check them out in reality.

TESTING AND ADJUSTING PERCEPTIONS AND ATTITUDES

We are concerned in this section with the identification of (a) certain devices which will expose problems in IDM groups and

(b) other devices which will enhance cooperation in those groups. Inevitably we shall be making suggestions pointing toward individual and group change; the change process itself, however, will be the basis of our discussion in Chapter 9.

Testing and adjusting mechanisms

Some methods that are useful in testing and adjusting the perceptual and attitudinal elements of the integrative process include:

1) *Leveling conferences.* There are a variety of techniques for eliciting the stereotypes and false images which parties have about each other. For example, Party A may be asked to list ways in which he would characterize Party B and the ways in which he thinks B would characterize him. After these lists are prepared, the parties meet together to compare their characterizations, which, by increasing their awareness of stereotypes, can enable them to combat the effect of such images.

2) *Pre-problem-solving meetings.* It may be useful for the parties to meet together to discuss possible differences of opinion and any other obstacles to effective problem solving. One way to gather data for such discussions is to ask each individual to list all of the obstacles to the attainment of a cooperative or integrative relationship which that person has experienced in relating to the other party. Each group's list of obstacles can then be compiled and can serve as the basis for discussion.

3) *Simulation exercises.* Since verbal statements of intent may not be borne out by behavior, it may be helpful for the parties to engage in exercises simulating the integrative process. The behavior demonstrated in such games is frequently the same as that which the parties would use in a real situation; thus, these exercises provide the parties with data concerning their likely behavior, as well as a basis for changing that behavior if it is judged to be dysfunctional. In addition, simulation exercises provide an opportunity to practice innovative behavior and to test its consequences.

4) *Sensitivity training.* Sensitivity training groups, also called encounter groups or T-groups, provide an opportunity

for participants to gain insights into their own behavior and to increase their understanding of others. Such training is also useful in developing skills associated with integrative processes: verbal skills, trusting behavior, cooperative approaches, etc. The usual training situation takes place in an isolated setting for a period of time that is generally either three or seven days, with the group composed of from eight to fifteen associates or strangers. Formats, conducted by a skilled training leader, vary according to the needs of the group but generally include an intensive discussion among the members, with a focus on interpersonal relations. Particularly useful for integrative purposes is the intragroup cohesion engendered by such training. Groups are usually marked by obvious differences among members in age, sex, status, culture, and the like. Such differences, if considered threatening, become barriers to cooperative effort. In the process of training, members generally become more aware of their similarities, they may even exaggerate such similarities as the group becomes more cohesive. Finally, however, the group may reach the point where it is sufficiently cohesive to value the differences among group members as resources for cooperative achievement.

5) *Exercising cooperative influence.* Some tactics of cooperation may be derived from *balance theory* (Newcomb, 1953; Heider, 1958), the basis of which is that a person prefers consistency in his perceptions and beliefs about another person. That is, if Party A feels that Party B is threatening, but B behaves in a nonthreatening manner, then such inconsistency must be removed in the mind of A, perhaps by changing A's feeling to one that B is not threatening after all. Walton and McKersie (1965, pp. 225–49) describe a number of ways that one party can influence the other to be more cooperative.

Methods of increasing cooperation

The following five guidelines enhance cooperation and decrease conflict between two opposing parties.

1) Cooperation will be increased when one party shares the likes and dislikes of another. This sharing will be emphasized if one party locates characteristics and interests which are held in common

by both parties. For example, a foreman and his subordinates may be moved to cooperate by a common dislike of an engineer who is re-arranging the work flow of the department. In much the same way, a group of people with high attraction to a charismatic leader are moved to cooperate, even though the members themselves may exhibit sharp differences in personalities or in personal interests. Likewise, similarity may be demonstrated by using language or frames of reference that are familiar to both parties. Or, superordinate goals may be identified; Sherif (1962, p. 11) defines superordinate goals as "goals which are compelling for all and cannot be ignored, but which cannot be achieved by the efforts and resources of one group alone."

Parties may also be joined by reminders of mutual success or progress. The usefulness of this technique is suggested by a phenomenon called the *Zeigarnik Effect*: that people tend to remember uncompleted tasks or unachieved goals more readily than completed tasks or achieved goals. For this reason it is helpful to consciously review previous successful experiences of cooperation between the parties.

Finally, cooperation is fostered by deemphasizing the differences between the parties. This effect may be demonstrated in "The Prisoner's Dilemma" (see Appendix). When the two parties in the game focus upon difference in earnings held by each, the incentive is to compete. On the other hand, when the parties see that each is gaining more through cooperation than through competition, they pay more attention to this mutual gain than to the differences in earnings.

2) Common association between two parties, even though it may not be judged positively or negatively, may induce positive feelings between them in a problem-solving situation. One method to increase mutuality is simply to increase interaction. While we have already seen that interaction can lead to some forms of conflict, there is also evidence that it leads to cohesion between the parties (Lott and Lott, 1965). Another way to increase such mutuality is to emphasize the common fate of the parties as it will be affected by the outcome of their association. Emphasizing similar backgrounds may also serve to bring the parties together. Perhaps the parties grew up in the same city, had the same kind of educational experiences, or have worked in similar occupations.

3) When a party becomes identified with or associated with something which is positively valued by the other party, cooperation may be achieved. For example, if a company representative helps a labor representative enhance his reputation among union members of the company, the labor negotiator might value the company man more

highly. Such help need not be costly to the helper, but it can be quite rewarding to the relationship.

4) A fourth method for increasing cooperative attitudes is for one party to acknowledge help received from the other party. A can influence B's attitude toward him by calling B's attention to the fact that B's actions helped A. In concrete terms, if a production manager thanks a sales manager for the benefits accruing to production from a sales training conference, the sales manager is likely to increase his positive feelings about the production manager. Walton and McKersie point out (p. 241) that by demonstrating to another that he has some control over one's own fate, one is establishing a basis for trust with the other party. One is saying, in effect, "I am willing to be influenced by you," that is, "I trust your judgment." Such vulnerability also establishes the basis for cooperative effort.

5) Another method for enhancing cooperation is for one party to dissociate himself from objects or situations which the other party dislikes. This can be done by disclaiming any role whatever, explaining that circumstances are beyond one's control, or by apologizing for an unfortunate occurrence and promising a change of behavior. For example, a union negotiator may disclaim responsibility for actions taken by union leaders which are judged negatively by the management negotiator; or A might explain an inability to continue with a meeting despite B's wish to do so on the grounds that A is due in traffic court and cannot be excused. B is less likely to feel negatively toward A than he would if the explanation were not given. Accusatory action should be avoided by both parties, because it will cause defensive reactions and reduce the likelihood of openness and problem solving. We dislike those we have harmed, therefore, A should avoid making Party B feel himself responsible for inflicting harm on A. If negative experiences have occurred, A may either avoid direct accusation of B or may say to B, "I know that this bad experience really is not your fault."

Ways of depersonalizing the situation

Finally, the depersonalization of issues increases the likelihood of cooperation among the parties involved. Efforts by parties to identify issues on which they disagree or to identify behaviors which lead to conflictive feelings can do much to encourage attitudes associated with problem solving. Put another way, where parties have a close personal relationship but are in a situation which is conflictive, their actions can either maintain, improve, or impair that closeness. By jointly studying the conflictive situation, they may engage in problem solving; by personalizing the situation they increase the distance between them.

One way to depersonalize the situation is to fight the antagonism rather than the antagonist. If parties hold conflicting values, both sides should attempt to understand those values and to find mutually satisfying outcomes rather than to associate the values with the other person and to fight that person. For example, the author recently observed an interaction between the sales manager and the chief of engineering in a small company which makes industrial equipment. The sales manager said, "All you care about is dreaming up new products. We just lost a $40,000 order from an auto producer who gave the order to a competitor. The auto company representative said that our standard items have deteriorated in quality and that they are unreliable. You had better figure out how to keep the quality of our bread-and-butter items or you will destroy the company." The chief of engineering said, "It is our new products that keep the company growing. If you would learn to sell the new equipment instead of operating in a rut, you would not have to worry about that old line." This situation contrasts the sales manager's value of reliability and efficiency in standard items and the engineer's value of innovation. By investigating the differences in their values and by asking "How can we derive the maximum benefit from standard items and from new equipment?" the conflictive situation could be turned into one of problem solving.

Another way to depersonalize an issue is to agree on a mechanism of agreement rather than on the issue itself. Thus, the parties may decide to flip a coin or to have the issue settled by an impartial judge. The difficulty with this method, however, is that it may result in a compromise rather than a mutually satisfactory solution. It allows the parties to hide behind the mechanism of solution instead of confronting the sources of disagreement between them. The parties dissociate themselves from the disagreement, but the outcome may not remove the conditions which fostered the conflictive situation.

Both parties in a dispute may also depersonalize their own relationship by dissociating themselves from the institutions which they represent. The parties may report that they are simply following orders or that they are acting for their organizations, with no personal animosity intended. The problem with this strategy, however, is that it reduces the incentive of the individuals involved to work toward mutually rewarding outcomes for their institutions. Such dissociation can keep the individuals on a cooperative basis personally, but prolong the institutional conflict.

It may be noted, in summary, that depersonalizing the problem will be most effective in promoting attitudes leading to problem solving where the parties address the issues or the source of antagonism without hiding behind conflict-resolving techniques like coin flipping and without avoiding responsibility for the groups which they represent.

NOTE ON EXPERIENTIAL LEARNING

Exercise 7 in the Appendix, "The Change of Work Procedure," demonstrates the difference in outcomes when conflict methods are used to settle a disagreement and when IDM is used to settle the same disagreement.

REFERENCES

Cohen, A. R. "The effects of individual self-esteem and situational structure on threat-oriented reactions to power." *Dissertation Abstracts* 14 (1954): 727-28.

Delbecq, A., and A. C. Filley. "A study of the weather satellite program management and organizational systems." In *Multidisciplinary Studies of the Social, Economic, and Political Impact Resulting from Recent Advances in Satellite Meteorology, Volume IV*, pp. 1-174. Space Science and Engineering Center, University of Wisconsin-Madison, 1972.

Deutsch, M. "Trust, worthiness and the F-scale." *The Journal of Abnormal and Social Psychology* 61 (1960): 138-40.

Filley, A. C., and R. J. House. *Managerial Process and Organizational Behavior*. Scott, Foresman, 1969.

Guetzkow, H., and J. Gyr. "An analysis of conflict in decision-making groups." *Human Relations* 7 (1954): 367-81.

Haythorn, W., A. Couch, D. Hoeffer, P. Langhem, and L. F. Carter. "The behavior of authoritarian and equalitarian personality groups." *Human Relations* 9 (1956): 57-74.

Heider, F. *The Psychology of Interpersonal Relations*. Wiley, 1958.

Janis, I. "Personality correlates of susceptibility to persuasion." *Journal of Personality* 22 (1954): 504-18.

Kagan, J., and P. H. Mussen. "Dependency themes on the TAT and group conformity." *Journal of Consulting Psychology* 20 (1956): 29-32.

Lott, A., and B. E. Lott. "Group cohesiveness as interpersonal attraction: A review of relationships with antecedent and consequent variables." *Psychological Bulletin* 64 (1965): 259-309.

Maier, N. R. *Psychology in Industrial Organizations.* Houghton Mifflin, 1973.

Newcomb, T. M. "An approach to the study of communicative acts." *Psychological Review* 60 (1953): 393-404.

Sherif, M., ed. *Intergroup Relations and Leadership.* Wiley, 1962.

Walton, R. E., and R. B. McKersie. *A Behavioral Theory of Labor Negotiations.* McGraw-Hill, 1965.

Later Stages
of Integrative
Decision Making

8

In the preceding chapter we discussed the relational conditions, perceptions, and attitudes that encourage the development of IDM. We now turn to the remaining steps in the integrative process: the problem definition, the search for solutions, and the consensus decision. As we pointed out in Chapter 1, the typical conflict situation is characterized by minimal problem definition, statements of two obvious and preferred solutions, and argumentation to determine which of the two solutions will be chosen. In contrast, the integrative process requires careful problem definition, an exhaustive and nonjudgmental search for alternative solutions, and a decision-making process based on evaluation and agreement. We shall consider each of these steps in turn.

PROBLEM DEFINITION

For integrative decision making to take place, (1) the ends, values, or goals of the parties must be identified, and (2) a mutually acceptable statement of those goals or of an obstacle to their attainment must be formulated. That is, the parties may have different goals, but each party must accept the stated goals of the other and not consider the problem solved until the solution is acceptable to both parties.

It is, of course, impossible to meet goals that are mutually exclusive, as in a game which is defined as having a winner and a loser, in the distribution of a fixed sum of money between two parties, or in the gain or loss of territory by two neighbors arguing over boundary lines. Yet experience with the integrative method indicates that many of these "fixed-sum" situations may be resolved with integrative processes. In addition, many situations assumed to be fixed sum are not.

In order to achieve a mutually acceptable statement of a problem, we provide the following six guidelines.

1) *Conduct a problem analysis to determine the basic issues.* When parties enter into a potentially conflictive situation, it is not uncommon for them to have two premature solutions as stated objectives. In other cases, one of the parties will have proposed a single solution, and the issue becomes one of supporting or not supporting that proposal. In still other cases, the parties will have stated an abstract objective such as "good communication" which has little specific meaning. In all such cases it is essential to find out the specific needs or desires of the parties by asking them to define specifically what they wish to accomplish with their proposed solutions or abstract objectives. This process may be repeated several times until a problem is defined which lends itself to a variety of solution strategies (Nadler, 1967).

The effects of this shift in focus to a specific statement of a problem is illustrated in a conflict situation in a Milwaukee hospital. The hospital, in an attempt to get more effective use of its nursing staff, defined a solution in terms of effective use of time; it implemented that solution by having a work-sampling procedure administered by an industrial engineer. A serious conflict resulted between the nursing staff and the administration regarding the fairness of doing the study and the acceptance or rejection of recommendations for improvement of time use.

Following the conflict, a consultant was asked to review the situation and to help the group resolve the conflict and proceed toward a viable solution to the problem. The consultant met with the parties and asked them what they wished to accomplish. The hospital administrators again stated that they wanted to improve the use of nursing time in order to increase nursing effectiveness. Both administrators and nurses were again asked what they hoped to accomplish. They responded that the objective was to increase the amount of time that nurses could spend with patients. The consultant asked the collective group what would be accomplished by this. Their reply was that more time spent with the patients would increase the quality of patient care in the hospital. The consultant asked one more time what would be accomplished. This time the administrators indicated that the average length of stay for patients was from eight to ten days and that the aim was to increase the speed of recovery and reduce the patient's in-hospital stay at the same or reduced cost. The problem definition was ended at this point, since it was acceptable to both the administration and the nursing staff and provided a convenient basis for a search for solutions.

2) *Avoid stating goals in the form of individual priorities.* In defining the problem, the parties may choose to group goals into categories indicating joint priorities, but should avoid stating the goals as individual priorities. The latter practice implies that the main objective is meeting the needs of one party and that any effort or value left over will go to the other party, rather than that the goals and the parties are valued equally.

For example, a married couple had argued for several years about where to take an annual vacation. The husband wanted to go camping and the wife wanted to go to a resort. In trying to arrive at an integrative solution, each stated the desired goals. The husband stated that he wanted to be in the woods and to go fishing. The wife stated that she wanted a clean bed to sleep in and a shower. Had the couple established a priority of first fishing and woods and, secondly, shower and bed, it would have implied that the husband's needs were more important than the wife's. By considering the needs as equal, equality of parties was ensured. The solution for this couple was to rent a Winnebago Motor Home and to travel to Yellowstone Park, parking the motor home in the woods.

3) *State the problem as a goal or as an obstacle rather than as a solution.* As emphasized in the first chapter, conflicts frequently occur when parties are solution-minded, rather than problem-minded. There is a tendency for parties to focus upon alternate solutions and then to argue about the means of implementing them, rather than to identify the end purpose to be achieved by following one of the solutions.

For example, a labor union's demand for a union shop may elicit a management counterargument. If, instead, the union describes its difficulty as one of controlling the membership, since nonunion employees benefit from union efforts without paying dues, then there are other solutions available besides the union shop agreement. Similarly, in the "Change of Work Procedure" (see Appendix), if the parties identify the problem merely as whether to use the new method or the old method, the result is likely to be win-lose or lose-lose. If, instead, the parties identify their needs as increasing production, keeping the team together, avoiding boredom, and keeping the boss happy, then there are several solutions which can meet those needs.

4) *Identify obstacles to goal attainment.* Problem definition must be specific; it should state the characteristics of the solution desired by the parties. In some cases, the easiest way to identify specific problems is to clarify obvious obstacles to goal attainment.

For example, consider a group of Catholics who banded together to plan and conduct their own religious services. After several years of unified and enthusiastic effort, the group was plagued with declining membership, apathy, and conflict. When members were asked to list their objectives in belonging to the group, the result was a list of abstract statements: "to live a good Christian life," "to maintain my belief," etc. Then, when the members were asked to "identify obstacles to the achievement of personal goals and satisfaction in being a member," the result was much more specific. Members identified subgroups and individuals who took control of the service, pointed out distractions caused by children playing during the service, expressed dislike for hymns chosen for services, etc. The first list provided little opportunity for problem solving, but the second elicited an agenda sufficiently specific to be used as a basis for direct improvements. In such cases, attention should be directed to those barriers or obstacles which can be changed.

5) *Depersonalize the problem.* In the last chapter we discussed the way in which problems can be identified without being accusatory or judgmental. To say "I do not have the same values as you" is far different from saying "Your values are wrong." The former is a fact; the latter a judgment. Similarly, to say "Let us look at the antagonism which we have experienced" encourages unified action by the parties in dealing with a depersonalied problem; to express anger is to personalize the situation.

Depersonalizing efforts are greatly enhanced by placing the needs and objectives of the parties into an impersonal format. The simple act of listing objectives on a flip chart or blackboard helps to shift attention away from the personalities involved to problems themselves. For both parties, the problem statement becomes the target to be defeated, rather than the opposing side.

6) *Separate the process of problem definition from the search for solutions and from the evaluation of alternatives.* Groups that achieve integrative solutions (a) spend proportionately more time in problem definition than do groups engaging in other solution methods and (b) separate the activities associated with problem definition from those associated with search behavior. Such a practice assures that the problem definition does not contain solutions, and increases the likelihood that the search stage will be more creative.

The need to separate problem definition from the search for solutions is particularly important when different parties engage in each of the two steps. The *problem* is always the necessary product of the parties in a conflictive situation, but *solutions* may be derived from sources other than the parties themselves. For example, where the parties to the problem are the clients of a social service agency and the agency, then the client group and agency staff obviously are best suited to define the problem. But in the search for solutions, on the other hand, outside experts may be added to the group to provide additional resources.

JOINT SEARCH FOR ALTERNATIVES

After defining the problem, the parties then should search for alternative solutions and should generate as many solutions as possible without evaluation.

While the affected parties are best suited to define the problem, anyone may offer a relevant solution. Outsiders may bring a fresh viewpoint, new information, or greater creativity to the search process. Thus, the parties may wish to expand the size of their group during the search for solutions.

Individuals are more productive in generating ideas, while interacting groups are more productive in evaluating ideas. The more people that are present, the greater the potential the group has for generating alternative solutions.

Several techniques may be used to generate possible solutions to a problem, including nominal groups, brainstorming, surveys, and discussion groups.

1) *Nominal groups.* In the nominal group process [1] people work in silence (nominally in the presence of each other) while they list possible solutions to the problem. The procedure may be described as follows: First, the specific statement of the problem is presented to the group. Then, members are asked to list all possible solutions to the problem that they can think of in a specified period of time without talking to each other. A period of ten minutes is generally suitable for this nominal listing phase. Members are urged to keep working for the full period to increase the likelihood of their exhausting all possibilities.

The next step calls for breaking down the large group into smaller subgroups of about five people. With someone acting as the recorder for each subgroup, its members read their solutions aloud, starting with the first solution and moving in round-robin fashion from one to another. The recorder writes each statement on a flip chart in sequence, from everyone's first statement to everyone's second statement, and so on.

The nominal process has several advantages: a) It permits everyone to work at the same time; b) by working in the presence of others, individuals tend to produce more solutions than they would working in isolation; c) it precludes the making of premature judgments concerning solutions; d) it depersonalizes the solutions, since they are removed from identification with individuals and are placed on a flip chart; and e) it is a relatively fast way to elicit ideas from as many as a hundred people, thus permitting the use of large groups for generating ideas. However, the nominal process is limited to the extent that it does not provide an opportunity for the idea of one party to stimulate the idea of another, as would be true where individuals verbalize their proposed solutions.

2) *Brainstorming.* Another approach to the search process calls for bringing a group of people together, presenting them with the problem, and then asking them to state as many solutions as they can think of while someone records the solutions. Members are cautioned against evincing any kind of judgment or evaluation as solutions are offered, for the point is to state any solution, no matter how impossible it seems, and to feel free to add to solutions proposed by

---

1. *For a detailed description of the nominal group process see A. Delbecq, A. Van de Ven, and D. Gustafson,* Group Techniques for Program Planning, *in this Series.*

others. As with nominal groups, the emphasis is upon an exhaustive search for solutions.

Brainstorming may be used with relatively large numbers of people. It preserves some order in the idea-generation process, while permitting the stimulus value of one member's ideas on another. As in nominal grouping, in brainstorming everyone works together in attacking the problem, and ideas are depersonalized by being listed. The chief difficulties with brainstorming are the opportunity for judgment or social pressure to take place and the necessary requirement that one person at a time propose solutions.

3) *Surveys.* It may be quite appropriate for the parties in the integrative process to conduct surveys of large numbers of people in their search for possible solutions. In such cases, each survey respondent is presented with the problem and asked to list as many suggestions as possible for dealing with it. While such surveys suffer from the lack of stimulus value gained by working in the presence of others, they take less of the respondents' time than would be used in attending a nominal group or brainstorming meeting.

4) *Discussion groups.* It may not be possible or desirable in all cases to have a large number of people respond to the problem. Instead, the parties directly concerned with the problem may wish to handle the search process themselves, possibly with the help of a few informed outsiders. Such might be the case when most outsiders would not fully understand the problem or when information required for the search restricts the number of people who could participate. At the same time, it should be noted that this unstructured search by a discussion group is open to difficulties which the three methods mentioned above preclude. Therefore, the following four guidelines are offered to promote the effectiveness of group discussions focusing on the search for alternative solutions to a problem.

a) *Avoid initial judgment or evaluation of proposed solutions.* As indicated above, it is important for the parties to save any considerations of the merits of solutions until the next stage of the integrative process. Even approving statements can be detrimental since they imply that suggestions not singled out for approval are not worth consideration. Experience has demonstrated that solutions which seem unrealistic or impossible at first can prove to be feasible upon further examination.

b) *Be exhaustive in searching for solutions.* In their desire to solve a problem or to settle a dispute, parties tend to accept the first solution that appears workable. It is necessary, therefore, for the parties to discipline themselves by allowing sufficient time for the search, continuing the process until all ideas have been generated. For example, Maier and Hoffman (1960) asked problem-solving groups to arrive at a solution, and then asked them to return to the task and to arrive at another solution. In fifty-four such groups, only 11.1 percent of the first solutions were integrative, while 42.6 percent of the solutions were integrative after additional search and consideration.

c) *Focus effort on the problem, not on the other party.* We have stressed repeatedly that the search process is a joint effort by everyone involved and that proposed solutions should not be regarded as the proprietary interest of either party. From this perspective, Walton and McKersie (1965, p. 152) discussed the effectiveness of labor-management relations:

One test of the extent to which the search process is really functioning is the extent to which the union and management abandon their respective offensive and defensive postures. In true problem solving the institutional roles are dropped and the identity of the participants becomes unimportant.

One aid in doing this, as mentioned previously, is to depersonalize the suggestions by listing them on a blackboard or flip chart. The resulting list is more likely to be viewed as a product of the group than as the property of any particular member.

d) *Bring in outside help.* As stated earlier, the addition of outsiders to the search process may add valuable resources. In some ways the experiences of the parties in their institutional settings can create blinders to creativity. Outsiders, unencumbered by such experiences, may actually view the situation in a new light and add to the group's problem-solving potential.

Once the search for alternative solutions to the problem is complete, the group can turn to the final step in the integrative process, that of making its evaluation and arriving at a decision.

EVALUATION AND CONSENSUS DECISION

Evaluation of possible solutions and arrival at an agreement which is acceptable to all of the parties is the final step in the integrative process.

Where the measures of quality and acceptability are clear and verifiable, the evaluation process entails little more than routine calculation.[2] Yet this frequently is not the case. Many decisions involve both factual, verifiable elements and elements which depend upon judgment and qualitative evaluation. For example, two business partners trying to agree on which of several suppliers to engage for materials in a production process will find that, in addition to elements of cost and proven quality, there are subjective elements which enter into their decision, such as the assurance of delivery dates, personal relations with suppliers, billing arrangements, etc. Judgments about what criteria to use for evaluation, about weighting of criteria, and about the application of such measures all constitute qualitative elements in the decision process.

The consensus process may also be used in situations without the aforementioned steps of the integrative process. For example, jury deliberations are in part restricted to a judgment about the guilt or innocence of a defendant. The jury must recall and reconstruct the facts, compare them to criteria associated with guilt or innocence, and make a judgment to which all jurors agree. In such cases the group emphasizes fact-gathering and logic as the basis for its judgment, and attends to emotional issues or personal needs only if they block group decision making.

The general atmosphere of a consensus group should be marked by the parties' unified attention to the problem, a relatively pleasant physical setting, and active participation by all members. Where parties do not reveal a cooperative spirit, they should go back and review and adjust their attitudes before attempting to arrive at a consensus decision.

Once the relational conditions, attitudes, and perceptions are appropriate, and the problem and its solutions are adequately defined, there are several guidelines which will help the parties arrive at a consensus decision:

2. *This section draws heavily from Maier (1963, 1973); Walton and McKersie (1965); and Guetzkow and Gyr (1954).*

1) *The range of solutions should be narrowed.* The focus should be upon selecting for consideration solutions that are good and acceptable, rather than bad or unacceptable. The former strategy is positive and is less likely to elicit defensive behavior, and it may be employed by asking each group member to select the three or four solutions that he considers most acceptable (Maier, 1973, p. 622). This process will eliminate solutions that are not supported by any group member and will also avoid the divisive effects of majority rule. The same method is often used to reduce the range of responses in nominal grouping discussed earlier in this chapter (p. 113).

2) *Solutions should be evaluated in terms of both quality and acceptability.* As we saw in Chapter 2, when the determining factors in a decision have nothing to do with the willingness of people to implement it or their concern as to its fairness, then initial attention can and should be directed to the rational evaluation of each alternative (Maier, 1963). Such a decision may need to be made, for example, about product pricing. Alternatively, when the quality of the solution and its acceptance by those who must make it work are important issues, then these issues should be considered simultaneously, for the best solution in terms of quality may not be superior if it lacks support. Finally, there are some cases in which acceptance of the decision is the overriding factor. In these cases, solutions should be evaluated in terms of their equity or acceptance. For example, a foreman with one football ticket that he wishes to give to any one of five subordinates would be well advised to determine the issue by asking the group to make the decision.

The composition of the evaluation group should parallel these concerns. Where the quality of the decision is paramount, then the evaluation group should be composed of individuals who can help in the analysis of alternatives by bringing in expert or informed knowledge. Where both quality and acceptance of the decision are important, the evaluation group should contain those with the essential knowledge and ability to determine how well accepted the decision will be. When acceptance is at issue, then the analysis of alternatives may be turned over to those who can judge its equity and fairness.

3) *Avoid the requirement that parties justify personal feelings or preferences.* There is no point in trying to change feel-

ings with some kind of intellectual argument or persuasion.
Nor is there much to be gained by asking parties to justify
their feelings. To do so merely creates a defensive posture
which does not lend itself to problem solving. Where an alternative under consideration is not acceptable to someone because
of his personal feelings or values, it is best to look for another
more favorable alternative. For example, a family group planning a dinner menu should look for food which meets the
needs and tastes of all the parties. To tell someone that he or
she should like stewed tomatoes when they have been rejected
is less effective than moving on to a consideration of other
kinds of food.

4) *It is helpful for the parties to agree on criteria for evaluation which may be dealt with individually and specifically.*
This is a common practice in the selection and/or evaluation
of employees in some organizations. The question of which
job candidate is "better" is considered by defining the characteristics of a good candidate and then comparing each application to those measures. The question of evaluating job
performance is resolved by outlining certain standards of job
performance and then applying those standards to present
employees.

In much the same way, when the parties find themselves
arguing about the likelihood of success, positions will frequently be expressed by statements that "It won't work," or
"It will work." In such cases, it is helpful to objectively determine the probability of success and to use this as a criterion
for evaluation.

5) *Consensus is most likely where there is little expression
of self-oriented needs.* Of course, no evaluation session can es-
cape the influence of personal biases. Individuals want personal
recognition, want to avoid being wrong or making mistakes,
have a proprietary interest in certain solutions, and have personal tastes or preferences which enter into the discussion.
Where such personal needs can be met in the course of a
discussion, the likelihood of consensus is greater. The disruptive possibility of seeking personal advantage may be reduced by
observance of group norms which emphasize that, for example,
individuals should not argue for their own positions but should
use logic and reason and consider other alternatives. Another

such norm is that members should overlook inconsistencies between another member's present and previous positions since calling attention to the inconsistencies merely serves to block change.

6) *Parties should review members' evaluations of alternatives periodically.* Related to the fifth guideline is the fact that personal evaluation of alternatives generally changes during a discussion, for the additional facts generated may cause parties to revise their estimates concerning the probability of success or the cost of implementation. It is important for all parties to be aware of such changes as they occur.

7) *Parties should avoid using agreement mechanisms which prevent open discussion of alternatives* As we discussed in Chapter 2, strategies such as voting, averaging, coin flipping, and the like are ways to avoid confrontation; and in that sense, they are something to hide behind. On the other hand, we have seen that open confrontation on issues may cause the parties to clarify the objectives and to search for creative solutions. As far as evaluation is concerned, the generation of facts and information is likely to be far less comprehensive when the parties resort to artificial mechanisms than when they are seeking consensus.

8) *Where the evaluation problem can be divided into parts, it may be helpful to establish smaller subgroups to deal with the parts.* In contrast to the joint search for alternatives, whose potential is advanced by large numbers of people, the evaluation and judgment stage benefits most from small-group interaction. Thus, movement into the third stage in the integrative process requires some limit on the group's size and composition. Larger groups increase the difficulty in achieving consensus, in attending to members' needs, and in achieving coordination. Thus, subgroups of five or seven people, containing representatives of both parties, may be used to help maintain trust and cooperation while dealing with part of the problem.

9) *Feelings of conflict should be resolved before continuing with the evaluation process.* It is not likely that consensus decision will be achieved when the parties become angry and accusatory and lack trust. As pointed out earlier, purely emotional conflict leads to separation of the parties or to agreements on the most trivial kinds of issues. The parties should return

to the review and adjustment of attitudes if such conditions threaten to disrupt consensus decision making.

The successful completion of the evaluation stage should leave the parties with a positive feeling toward the outcome and toward each other. All parties should have experienced feelings of success in the outcome and should exhibit high commitment to the agreement. In many cases the actual quality of the decision may be expected to be better than the quality of an individual decision. Experience with the methods demonstrates the rewards: quality, commitment, and understanding. The costs are, of course, time and energy and perhaps some frustration—all of which seem rather small prices to pay for win-win outcomes.

SOME EXAMPLES OF INTEGRATIVE DECISION MAKING

Throughout this book we have employed examples of integrative methods: the prison staff deciding on appropriate attire for guards, the couple making use of an air-conditioned room, the creative arrangement of serving coffee in an office—all could have been handled by win-lose or lose-lose methods, but each was resolved with an integrative solution. Let us consider some other examples which follow the integrative method in whole or in part.

Father and son at the dinner table

The first situation which we pose is hypothetical, but it serves as a convenient model of the integrative method. Consider a father and his son seated at the dinner table. The food has been served and the father notices that the son has failed to eat his spinach. The father says, "Eat your spinach." The son says, "I don't like spinach." This conflictive situation may be handled in several ways.

Some win-lose outcomes might be expected if, for example, the father says, "Look, damn it, I am your father; I am older and wiser than you are; I pay the bills around here. Now, eat your spinach." Or, if the father says, "Eat your spinach," the son might say, "If I eat my spinach, I'll throw up!" Compliance by the son in the first case would leave him frustrated; compliance by the father in the second instance might well leave him unhappy.

Some lose-lose outcomes might occur if the father says, "Look, just eat part of your spinach." If the son complies, then neither the father nor the son gets complete satisfaction. Or, the father might bribe the son by saying, "If you will eat your spinach, then I'll take you to the baseball game." In this instance it costs the father extra to get the son to do something he does not want to do. (Additional money payments to wage earners for unpleasant work afford similar examples.)

An integrative outcome might occur if the father were to say, "Look, son, we are fighting with each other; let's try to find out what we both want. What I really want is for you to have nourishing food." The son might say, "What I want is food that tastes good." Thus, the problem statement for father and son is: what kinds of food can be served that 1) are nourishing and 2) taste good? At this point the father and the son could prepare a list of foods and then evaluate the list according to the two criteria. If either party feels that something must be done about the portion of spinach, then it too could be the basis for problem solving. When the issue is role-played with real people, the usual outcome is for them to feel that eating or not eating the spinach is not important if the basic problem is solved.

Unilateral union program of training in problem solving

The second example illustrates the way in which some of the relational conditions, perceptions, and attitudes in a labor-management relationship were handled unilaterally by a union. In this case, the Amalgamated Meat Cutters and Retail Food Store Employees Union (Local 342) and a supermarket employers' association, after serious bitterness in earlier negotiations, attempted to bargain in a more rational manner (Stern and Pearse, 1968). This shift to problem solving on a nonaccusatory basis met with some success among the bargaining representatives but was viewed with suspicion by their constituencies.

In an attempt to increase the integrative skills of the union members, and particularly to increase their understanding and to gain their support for integrative bargaining through union representatives, the union, with the help of behavioral science consultants, began an extensive program 1) to teach elected negotiating committees the theory and skills associated with integrative methods, 2) to communicate realistic contract needs to the broad union membership, and 3) to take the time pressure out of preparation for negotiations and at the same time solicit the ideas of everyone about contract problems.

The first step in the program was a four-day sensitivity training lab designed for officers and union representatives. Included in the lab was an extensive discussion of perceptions about the role of a good union representative. Next, the various forms of conflict resolution were presented and discussed in the language of supermarket and meat department operations. Further efforts were directed at a sharing of attitudes and feelings among the group and a development of better interpersonal skills. Finally, the group discussed their feelings about how union meetings were being run and how local officers handled negotiations and then prepared a list of recommended improvements. The result was a clarification and adjustment of relational conditions both between the union and management and among groups within the union. Perceptions and attitudes were subjected to reality testing through identification of roles and feedback about personal feelings. As a result, union officers reported a reduction in conflict among staff members, an increase in cooperation among geographic or regional offices, and greater participation by representatives in decision making.

The next step in the program was a two-day workshop on communication skills in preparation for a shop stewards' conference. The workshop focused upon role-playing interactions as well as upon communication in union meetings between union officers and the rank and file. The skills gained were practiced in the steward conference through small-group discussions of union issues and problems.

A few months later three two-day meetings of union officers and representatives were scheduled. The primary emphasis in these meetings was upon problem-solving skills as they applied directly to forthcoming contract renewals. Members participated in exercises which demonstrated group and individual risk taking, and they completed a form indicating individual needs and role choices. Then, they simulated bargaining and problem solving by taking the roles of managers in a company setting, and later by taking the roles of union and management representatives in a simulated bargaining setting.

Following this, the union entered into actual negotiations with management. Union officers reported that the training had resulted in greater involvement by union groups in setting goals, more support and understanding of union positions by the rank and file, strong ratification of the new contract and support for the officers, and a favorable contract settlement. Judging from the report, the skills developed through the training did much to eliminate conflict and to promote cooperation in the union. Since the stimulus for the training in the first place was a desire for integrative methods instead of conflictive bargaining between union and management, we may also suppose that management involvement was improved as well.

Influencing a domestic conflict

The following is an example which came from one of my students It is presented as it was written. It illustrates how a focus on two solutions can preclude the definition of goals and the feelings generated by win-lose methods of conflict resolution. The student's intervention clearly depersonalized the problem and moved through the steps in the integrative method.

"This exercise in integrative decision making occurred while I was home for Easter vacation. My father is currently adding a large kitchen-dining room to our house. The addition is the request of my mother who has outgrown her old kitchen, and in one sense dad is building it according to her specifications. My father is a carpenter, however, so his work must be up to his own professional standards. Often, mother's specifications and dad's standards are at odds. The period of construction up until vacation had been marked by several disagreements. These disagreements had been settled by compromise in some instances, and in others a flat refusal on the part of one of my parents to be dissuaded. I saw that mother was less happy about the addition than she was before the work started. Dad was beginning to feel railroaded and displeased about the way things were going. In short, they were both frustrated losers.

"When I arrived dad had just finished the construction of the kitchen cabinets. He had used top-grade pine and a top-grade birch for the doors. He had spent quite a bit of time and effort in their construction and felt he had really done a good job. We all agreed that the cabinets were beautifully constructed. The question now was—what kind of finish to use on them?

"Mother had very definite ideas on the subject. She wanted them painted a dark brown. This she said would look very good with the avocado tile flooring they had already purchased. Besides she had been very impressed with a neighbor's kitchen which had dark brown cabinets and by a similar kitchen in Better Homes and Gardens. Dad wouldn't hear of such an idea. Dark brown paint would cover up not only the beautiful natural grain in the expensive wood but also cover up the fine detail and the great care he took in the construction. He was outraged that mother could splotch brown paint on his cabinets and said he had decided on clear-varnishing the cabinets so the natural grain and color could show. Neither appeared willing to budge, and I could see that a solution reached through past strategies would really add to the tension and unhappiness already in the family.

"Determined to keep things as cool as possible during my vacation I persuaded my parents to sit down and try something I had been introduced to in school in order to solve the cabinet finish problem. I told them it was possible to decide on a finish that would dissatisfy neither of them. They didn't believe me and, in fact, I was none too confident myself. As a first step I asked them to think of their goals regarding how they wanted the cabinets to look. At first the answers were variations on two themes, "painted brown" on the one hand and on the other "clear-varnished." This was a crucial point and I explained that these really weren't goals but rather just a means of reaching their real goals. This was the toughest point because I had to get them to see that they were each settled on and arguing for their own particular solution without really knowing what their goals were and without searching for other solutions. Finally, I got them problem oriented and got the following lists of goals from them:

Mother	*Father*
1. Cabinets to go with floor.	1. Finish that shows grain.
2. Cabinets like neighbor's and in magazine.	2. Finish that doesn't cover his craftsmanship.
3. Cabinets that don't show dirt and are easy to clean.	3. Cabinets he can be proud to show his friends.
4. Cabinets she can be proud of as she shows them to her friends.	

"We discussed each of the goals and what they meant in terms of the required solution. Cabinets to go with the avocado floor could be any of several red, green, or brown hues. Cabinets that don't show grease and dirt will necessarily be a dark shade. We looked at the magazine layout together and mother admitted much of the look of the cabinets she admired was due to the antiqued copper hinges and handles. She also said that the cabinets didn't actually have to be as dark as the ones in the magazine to look okay. Dad's goals pointed up the need for some type of varnish or natural finish and ruled out enamels.

"A consensus solution came soon enough. A natural oil wood stain in some medium-dark color would match the floor, not show dirt and grease, and look good with the copper hinges and handles. The oil stain soaks into the wood and the natural grain shows through. With several coats of clear varnish over the stained wood dad's craftsmanship would be shown off to good advantage, and with the addition of the copper accessories the magazine look would be achieved. After trying several stains on scrap wood they settled on a medium-oak shade. Out of respect and gratitude for my problem-solving ability, I was allowed to do the finishing job."

REFERENCES

Delbecq, A., A. Van de Ven, and D. Gustafson, *Group Techniques for Program Planning*. Scott, Foresman, 1975.

Maier, N. R. *Problem-Solving Discussions and Conferences: Leadership Methods and Skills*. McGraw-Hill, 1963.

Maier, N. R. *Psychology in Industrial Organizations*. Houghton Mifflin, 1973.

Maier, N. R., and L. R. Hoffman. "Quality of first and second solutions in group problem solving." *Journal of Applied Psychology* 44 (1960): 278-83.

Nadler, G. *Work Systems Design: The IDEALS Concept*. Irwin, 1967.

Stern, I., and R. F. Pearse. "Collective bargaining: A union's program for reducing conflict." *Personnel* 45 (1968): 61-72.

Walton, R. E., and R. B. McKersie. *A Behavioral Theory of Labor Negotiations*. McGraw-Hill, 1965.

Changing Conflict Resolution Skills and Behavior

9

In this final chapter we shall be concerned with identifying those conditions which are generally present when individuals and groups change their established patterns of behavior. In doing so, we shall also suggest the role of the change agent—the one who wishes to help others change their behavior from conflictive to problem-solving. As we have emphasized throughout this book, each person develops well-practiced patterns of behaviors which are difficult to change. In general, future behavior is best predicted by past behavior—that is, circumstances being equal, people will go on doing what they have always done. If an individual has typically been compliant, then he will continue to be compliant; if self-seeking, he will likely continue to be self-seeking; if compromising, he will continue to pursue a lose-lose strategy. This picture is neither cynical nor pessimistic—it is simply realistic.

Yet there are cases in which individuals do change; they change their attitudes, their behavior. Certain conditions are typically associated with these cases of change, and by knowing what those conditions are, a person can increase the likelihood that he can effect a desired change in his behavior.

Where an individual, perhaps the reader, wants to change another individual, the situation is even more complicated, for here the change agent must depend upon the willing cooperation of the person being changed. The change agent merely helps another person to change. His tools for this task are neither argument nor persuasion; rather, they are, metaphorically, a mirror, a picture, and a prayer. By using the mirror (for example, feedback or an experiential exercise), the change agent provides the person with facts regarding his behavior. By using the picture (for example, a demonstration of new behavior), the change agent provides alternatives for the person's present behavior. And by means of the prayer (for example, a proposed sense of direction) the change agent may help the person move toward specific goals.

CHANGES IN KNOWLEDGE, ATTITUDES, AND SKILLS

In describing the change process, it is useful to identify the variables of change. As Robert House (1967) points out, the usual change variables are (a) knowledge, (b) attitudes, (c) skills, (d) individual behavior, and (e) organizational or group behavior. Change in any or all of the first three—knowledge, attitudes, and skills—may not entail a resultant alteration in behavior, partly because the social and organizational context in which the individual operates may make it difficult for him to change. That is, pressures exerted by a boss, peers, and subordinates, coupled with the rewards provided by the organization in which the individual functions, may interfere with the change process.

The relationships between the kinds of change and the conditions which support change are also suggested by House. Summarizing his findings, we see in Figure 9–1 that an increase in knowledge depends upon one's personal characteristics, motivation, and ability to learn. Attitude and skill changes, however, depend not only on the motivation and ability of the person undergoing change, but also upon the training or change process used. For example, while a person may gain knowledge by merely reading a book or hearing a lecture, those two processes might have little effect on the person's values or beliefs. Processes which alter beliefs often spring from deep and intimate involvement with one's own feelings and the feelings of others.

Let us consider what happens when skills and attitudes change. First, individuals try to keep some degree of balance and consistency between what they believe and how they act; they try to keep what goes on inside themselves consistent with their external actions. Second,

FIGURE 9–1.   Relationships Between the Kinds of Change and the Conditions that Support Change. Adapted from R. J. House, *Management Development: Design, Evaluation, and Implementation*. Ann Arbor: Bureau of Industrial Relations, The University of Michigan, 1967. Reprinted by permission.

To Change →		Knowledge Change	Attitude Change	Skill Change	Individual Change in Behavior	Organizational Change in Behavior
Control For	Participant Characteristics	X	X	X	X	X
	Change Process		X	X	X	X
	Leader and Group Support				X	X
	Organizational Rewards and Sanctions					X

since both internal and external factors are usually involved in change, one may start the change process with either the internal components or with external behavior. As stated earlier, these situations can be observed in various schools of psychotherapy; some therapeutic approaches attempt to restructure what goes on inside the person, while others start by altering external behavior. Finally, for a change in attitudes and skills to be successful, a new balance between internal beliefs and external behavior must be achieved. If the change process starts with altering one's belief system, then a change in behavior must follow. Otherwise, the balance may be restored by keeping the old behavior and returning to previous beliefs and attitudes. Similarly, if the change process starts by altering behavior, then the internal components must also be adjusted. In the present context, a person wishing to change attitudes and skills must believe that problem solving is possible and desirable, and he must know how to practice the skills associated with problem solving.

Figure 9-1 further indicates that an individual is not likely to attempt to use the new knowledge, attitudes, and skills unless there is social support for the new behavior. An individual's boss, friends, family, peers, subordinates, and other valued people must accept or encourage the change in behavior. Herein lies a dilemma. We generally expect others to behave in a predictable manner and to some extent discourage change. Even though someone may attempt to change his behavior for the better, we will do some things which punish the attempted new behavior and reward the old. Thus, another kind of balance must be established between how the individual behaves and how others expect him to behave.

Finally, people tend to do those things for which they are evaluated and rewarded. A change in problem-solving behavior, once the other change steps have been met, will be more likely to occur and persist if supported by pay, promotion, and other reward systems. Figure 9-1 indicates that for change to take place among large numbers of people in an organization, the formal reward system of the organization must be in balance with the change. For example, if an organization expects to utilize interdepartmental problem-solving groups, then it must see that participants are evaluated positively for their work (Luke et al., 1973).

THE PROCESS OF INDIVIDUAL CHANGE IN BEHAVIOR

Although the best predictor of an individual's behavior is likely to be his past behavior in a similar situation and people seem to be "frozen" into fixed patterns of response in given situations, we have seen instances of people changing their behavior in some permanent way; and whether we are discussing a change in leadership style, problem-solving behavior, drinking behavior, or even religious affiliation, we can perceive certain characteristics to be associated with the change process.[1]

We shall discuss these characteristics under three general

1. This section draws heavily from G. W. Dalton, "Influence and Organizational Change," in Organizational Behavior Models, Comparative Administration Research Institute Series No. 2, © 1970 by the Bureau of Economic and Business Research, Kent State University. Also reprinted in A. C. Bartlett and T. A. Kayser (eds.), Changing Organizational Behavior, Prentice-Hall, Inc., Englewood Cliffs, New Jersey, © 1973.

headings: 1) unfreezing, 2) trial with new behavior, and 3) refreezing. Kurt Lewin (in Newcomb and Hartley, 1965) is credited with labeling these characteristics, and the words fit nicely. The first, *unfreezing*, is a loosening of the fixed pattern of behavior. The second, *trial with new behavior*, refers to a change in the old way of doing things. The third, *refreezing*, suggests a permanent pattern of new behavior, such that the best predictor of behavior will be the "refrozen" behavior.

Unfreezing

The first stage in the process of altering behavior is concerned with the breaking down of old patterns, establishing a sense of direction for change, and moving toward some new set of behaviors. The elements associated with unfreezing are as follows:

1) *Feelings of stress and tension.* A key motivator for change is a feeling of discomfort with old behavior. Individuals enter therapy because of dissatisfaction with their way of living; they may engage in serious religious change because of acute guilt or unhappiness; they may, if they occupy managerial positions, alter their leadership style because they realize that the old way is creating serious problems. Similarly, people who are uncomfortable about the results of their usual behavior in conflict situations may be ready to alter their conflict resolution style.

Put another way, persuasion, logic, force, or threats will fail to effect change in a person unless that person is motivated to seek a new method of behaving through dissatisfaction with the old one. For the change agent, then, there are two avenues for intervention: First, he can heighten the other person's awareness of behavioral consequences; and second, he can wait until tension is created in the other person. The former avenue may be pursued, for example, by having the person participate in an exercise to demonstrate the effects of cooperative or competitive behavior, in the course of which he sees that his competitiveness creates a win-lose situation. He may say to himself, "This is exactly what I do in the real world, and it explains why I have had difficulty in working with others."

Creation of the necessary tension for change may be achieved by setting up situations which cause a person to confront his own style of behavior. On the other hand, the change agent may find it necessary to wait until tension occurs in an existing situation before helping an individual (or group) to change behavior. Meanwhile, he may wish to alert the person or group to the availability of alternative behavior—saying, in effect, "If you feel that your current behavior is giving you what you want, fine. But if you ever feel that your behavior is not effective and you would like to develop some alternate skills, I shall be happy to help you." Having been alerted to the fact that problem-solving behavior is associated with creativity, job interest, and co-operation, the individual or group experiencing tension with the effects of win-lose or lose-lose methods may eventually seek the change agent's help.

2) *The presence of a trusted change agent.* As suggested above, the unfreezing process will often take place through the efforts of a trusted helper· People who undergo a change often do so through the efforts of a minister, therapist, consultant, staff specialist, or other neutral supportive individuals. The exact reasons why these individuals are effective in the role of change agent are not entirely clear, but one reason they are effective is that they are expected to be. Thus, we have a self-fulfilling prophecy—if I believe that you can teach me behavior which will make me happier or more productive, then to some extent what you teach me will make me feel happier or more productive.

Another reason for the change agent's effectiveness is his awareness of behavioral consequences, plus the ability to suggest alternatives which will improve behavior and its outcomes. For example, if a manager says, "I find that I always give in to what other people want to do and I spend my life sacrificing my needs to the needs of others," the change agent can demonstrate alternative behaviors which may not have been apparent to the manager.

Another probable reason for the effectiveness of the change agent is his neutrality in the conflict situation. By being open and honest, by being descriptive and not judgmental, and by accepting the person or group without prejudice, the change agent establishes the fact that the proposed change is in the interest of the person or group.

Chris Argyris (1970) has suggested the characteristics asso-ciated with an effective intervention by a change agent: (a) the establishment of valid information, (b) the development of inde-pendence on the part of the client, and (c) the development of client commitment to change. These guidelines imply that the change agent and the client must perceive conditions as they actually exist through reality testing. Further, the change agent must behave in a manner which helps the client become a fully functioning individual, making his own choices and being responsible for his own behavior. When the client determines his own solutions to problems, he is more likely to achieve and maintain lasting changes.

3) *Acceptance of past behavior.* Unfreezing is also associated with personal acceptance and responsibility for old patterns of behavior. As noted in Chapter 5, people have a tendency to take credit for behaviors and outcomes which are positive, successful, and pleasant but to blame failures or unpleasant experiences on conditions outside themselves. Thus, a manager may say, "I know that my subordinates do not like to be ordered about, but what can I do? I do not have time for problem solving." In that case he is attributing the dissatisfaction of his subordinates to conditions beyond his control. An alternative would be for the manager to say, "I behave in a manner which does not allow time for problem solving and the result of my behavior is dissatisfaction of my subordinates." By *owning* or taking responsibility for his own behavior, the manager would permit work on the problem of how to change that behavior.

4) *Awareness of alternatives.* Common notions about resistance to change often ignore the fact that there is no point in giving up present behavior if new behavior is unknown or uncertain. The unfreezing process is greatly aided by the awareness of the person or group of any alternatives available. An effective change agent will provide an array of possible alternatives to the individual or group whose behavior is causing problems, because those who have placed themselves in a corner must have plenty of doors to walk through.

5) *Social support for change.* Ideally, the unfreezing process is accompanied by support for changed behavior by others who are valued. Where such support is not forthcoming, the individual must at least be removed from a situation which encourages the old behavior.

It is not uncommon for people to encourage undesirable or unrewarding behavior in others, just because they are used to responding to them in a certain way and do not know how to deal with them differently. The subtlety of this phenomenon was brought home to the author in his experiences with two alcoholic friends. The first friend, who has had a serious drinking problem for years, would call or visit me at all hours of the day or night when drunk and in need of a friend. I would always greet him and talk with him, feeling that he was a valued friend but also wishing that he would stop drinking. When I described this situation to the second dry alcoholic friend he said, "Why do you encourage him to drink?" I said, "I don't. I tell him that I wish he would stop." The second friend then said, "If you want him to stop drinking, say to him, 'Look, you are my close friend and I value you greatly, but I won't talk to you when you are drunk, only when you are sober.'" I had unintentionally been encouraging my friend's drinking behavior by my actions.

Trial with new behavior

After the unfreezing of old behavior, the next step is for individuals seeking change to try an alternative behavior and determine its consequences. There are two important elements in this step:

1) *Success with new behavior.* A change process that is likely to be successful is one in which attempts at new behavior are perceived as successful by the person or group making the attempts. When new behavior is tried and is not judged as successful, then it will not be used. But when new behavior is tried and is found to be rewarding, then the chance that it will continue is increased. There is no more potent support for changed behavior than the realization by the individual or group experimenting with it that "It works."

Experiences of success with new behavior are so important that they should take place under controlled conditions in the beginning. A change agent who wishes to establish problem-solving behavior will, for example, have individuals or groups participate in simulations or experiential learning situations which have predictable outcomes. By knowing that an exercise will easily demonstrate successful utilization of problem solving skills, the change agent reinforces the knowledge, attitudes, and skills necessary to deal with more complicated "real-world" situations.

The use of controlled situations is something like the use of drug therapy with alcoholics. Drugs which reduce the client's anxiety (associated with a craving for alcohol) and drugs which cause nausea if he takes a drink enable the client to experience nondrinking behavior. His feelings of success via this support make it easier for him to take the unsupported step later. Similarly, individuals with a long history of unsuccessful work experience should be helped to see that their efforts will actually lead to acceptable levels of performance. This experience may be achieved by training in simulated work settings where some of the actual pressures for pace and quality have been removed. Success in an initially controlled training environment begets success in real life situations; winning begets more winning.

2) *Experiences in an isolated setting.* As suggested above, it is often easier to provide successful trial with new behavior in situations which are removed from the multiple pressures and cues of everyday life. It is no accident that change processes often take place in institutional settings—a school, a hospital, a training facility, a therapeutic facility. In such situations, individuals or groups have an opportunity to practice their new behavior without the distraction of cues which evoke old behavior and in the presence of others undergoing the same experience. It is far easier to work through the difficulties of trying new behavior when one knows that others are having the same difficulties.

For this reason, change agents are well advised to remove clients from their regular environment if that environment is antithetical to successful trial with new behavior. Although the regular work or living environment is important in the maintenance of change, the pattern of behavior must be believed, known, and applied if the likelihood of change is to be great. For example when members of a social service agency attempt to develop problem-solving skills in the office environment, cues, distractions, and previous associations will strongly affect trials with new behavior. It may be more desirable to take the group to a motel, college, or other location for the initial learning experiences. Practiced, successful behavior will make refreezing into a new pattern much easier.

Refreezing

If the change process is to be successful, the new behavior must be refrozen. Dalton (1970) suggests several characteristics that accompany refreezing:

1) *A change from general to specific objectives.* Initial attempts to change behavior are often described in general terms—to do better work, to be happier, to be a better supervisor. But for refreezing to be successful, the person or group will need to identify specific behavioral objectives. Instead of saying, "I want to make better use

of my time," the manager should now say, "At the start of each day, I will identify the five tasks which, when completed, will have made my day productive." Instead of saying, "I want to increase my skill in conflict resolution," the manager should now say, "When I find myself arguing with someone about two solutions, I will stop and ask each of us to write down the needs, goals, or values which we hope to achieve with those two alternatives." Instead of saying, "I want to be a better parent," the father should say, "When issues arise in our family that affect all of us, I will ask for a family meeting in which problems can be resolved by consensus." In this manner, specific behavioral objectives are established which describe behavior to be accomplished.

2) *Personal ownership of new behavior.* Where refreezing takes place the new behavior is "owned" by the people who have gone through the change process. It is not identified with the change agent or others; it is now the personal behavior of the parties. For example, the author recently installed a system of management by objectives (MBO) in a large printing company. In the beginning, managers would occasionally describe the program as "your (my) system" or the "MBO system that you are installing." Now, when I visit the company managers will say, "Filley, we need some improvements in the forms we are using in our system." Or, "We need your help in extending our system to the foreman level." The managers have clearly taken the responsibility for a system of management which is their own.

3) *A change to higher self-esteem.* In line with our assumption that the change process is one of moving to new behavior which will be more rewarding, for refreezing to take place the actual experiences with new behavior must be viewed as more rewarding. Pride, satisfaction, and self-esteem should accompany the new behavior. Whether the change concerns problem-solving skills, leadership style, drinking behavior, marital relations, or some other subject, refreezing will depend in part on the personal sense—objective and subjective—that the new condition or behavior is better than the old.

4) *New social relations.* The web of social relations in which an individual operates plays an important part in maintaining his behavior. Roles and norms are defined in groups, and persons violating such roles and norms are punished. In addition, as we have pointed out, unexpected behavior in a person creates some anxiety in those who have grown to expect him to behave in a certain way. Thus, a group does much to maintain the old behavior of someone wishing to change. If new behavior is to be refrozen, one or more social conditions will generally be altered to support the new behavior. In some cases,

the individual will establish a new set of social relations with roles and norms different from those operating in his old web of social relations. For example, the alcoholic who has stopped drinking may find friends who have also established a nondrinking pattern of behavior. Or, a supervisor who has developed his or her problem-solving skills may change positions from a job in an organization based upon a dominance-submission approach to management to one which seeks to involve groups of people in decision making.

Another way to refreeze a change in behavior through social maintenance of such behavior is to ensure that the maintenance group adopts the same changes with respect to its roles and rules. For example, Masters and Johnson (1970) point out the difficulty in treating one member of a married couple for some form of sexual inadequacy. However it starts, the sexual dysfunction becomes a pattern to which both parties contribute and which both parties maintain. If such dysfunction is to be dealt with, both parties must be part of the therapeutic process to alter behavior and both parties are important in the establishment of new patterns of behavior.

Finally, in some cases, new social relations may be developed merely by altering expectations within an individual's social network concerning his new behavior. It may be sufficient to alert or sensitize a group to adjust its role expectations in light of one of its member's new behavioral objectives. Such adjustments are probably best done by design rather than being left to chance. For example, a change agent working with a manager who is altering his supervisory style might meet with the manager's superiors and his immediate subordinates to discuss expected changes and to clarify how they can help the manager to change.

Whatever refreezing method is selected, success will depend importantly on the change, help, and support the social group provides the individual seeking to maintain new behavior.

A POSTSCRIPT

The preceding discussion, as well as the contents of this book in general, should suggest that IDM is in no sense a panacea or magic cure. Indeed, this approach to problem solving will not always work, nor is it always warranted. The motivation to use IDM will depend upon several factors. First, one must be confident that it can be employed adequately. Since such confidence depends upon having the necessary knowledge and skills, we have tried to state carefully and clearly the methods to be used. In addition, since such confidence depends upon firsthand experience in using IDM successfully, we have included exercises in an appendix by which readers can demonstrate its feasibility.

Second, one must see that the IDM approach to problem solving results in better decisions, greater acceptance of decisions, and reduced hostility among the concerned parties. If this connection between behavior and outcomes is not seen as clear and achievable, or if these kinds of goals are not desired, then it is not likely that the IDM method will or should be applied.

Integrative methods are simply techniques for handling conflictive situations in ways that are different from those practiced by many people. While no discussion can be entirely value-free, we have attempted to avoid passing moral judgment on the decision-making methods presented. The evaluation of integrative methods as "good" or "bad," of course, is up to the reader, together with the assessment of goals in whose pursuit they may be applied.

The effort and purpose of writing this book will have been met if the reader understands the methods presented and tries to apply them. If the experience gained in their application is favorable, then the reader may well continue to use them. If the experience is not favorable, well—fair enough. But if the reader does not test them out in his or her own experience, we may both have lost.

REFERENCES

Argyris, C. *Intervention Theory and Method: A Behavioral Science View.* Addison-Wesley, 1970.

Dalton, G. W. "Influence and organizational change." In *Organizational Behavior Models, Comparative Administration Research Institute Series No. 2.* Bureau of Economic and Business Research, Kent State University, 1970.

House, R. J. *Management Development.* Bureau of Industrial Relations, University of Michigan, 1967.

Lewin, K. "Group decision and social change." In *Readings in Social Psychology,* E. E. Maccoby, T. M. Newcomb, and E. L. Hartley, eds., pp. 197–211. Holt, Rinehart, & Winston, 1958.

Luke, R. A., Jr., P. Block, J. M. Davey, and V. R. Averch. "A structural approach to behavioral change." *Journal of Applied Behavioral Science* 9 (1973).

Masters, W. H., and V. E. Johnson. *Human Sexual Inadequacy*. Little, Brown, 1970.

Appendix:
Exercises

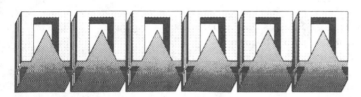

EXERCISE 1
GROUP DECISION MAKING

By eliciting individual and group responses to factual statements based on a simple story, the following exercise (employing concepts developed in Chapter 2) demonstrates the frequent superiority of group decisions over individual decisions. The result of this exercise should be a heightened awareness of the potential of group problem-solving methods.

Goal

1. To demonstrate the forms of conflict-resolving behavior.
2. To compare and contrast the effects of individual and group decision making.
3. To demonstrate the effect of consensus methods on group problem solving.

Group conditions

Any number of people divided into small groups of four or five.

139

Time required

Fifteen minutes for individual responses. Thirty minutes for group consensus.

Materials needed

Worksheet for each individual
Worksheet for each group
Pencils
Flip chart, newsprint, or blackboard
Marker pens or chalk

Physical setting

Flexible seating in one large room so that small groups may work together.

Process

A. Each individual is given a copy of the worksheet and is told that he has fifteen minutes to read the story and answer the eleven questions about the story. Each person may refer to the story as often as needed but may not confer with anyone else. Each person should circle "T" if the answer is clearly true; "F" if the answer is clearly false; or, "?" if he cannot tell from the story whether the answer is true or false.

B. After fifteen minutes the trainer announces that each small group will make the same decisions using group consensus. No one should change his answers on the individual worksheet, and the answers to the group decisions are to be placed on the group worksheets which are distributed to each group.

The following ground rules for group decisions should be read and posted by the exercise leader:

1. Group decisions should be made by consensus. It is illegal to vote, trade, average, flip a coin, etc.
2. No individual group member should give in only to reach agreement.
3. No individual should argue for his own decision. Instead, he should approach the task using logic and reason.
4. Every group member should be aware that disagreements may be resolved by facts. Conflict can lead to understanding and creativity if it does not make group members feel threatened or defensive.

C. After thirty minutes of group work, the exercise leader should announce the correct answers. Scoring is based on the number of correct answers out of a possible total of eleven. The trainer should announce that each individual is to score his own individual worksheet and that someone should score the group-decision worksheet. He should then call for:
   1. The group-decision score in each group
   2. The average individual score in each group
   3. The highest individual score in each group
D. Responses should be posted on the tally sheet. Note should be taken of those groups in which the group score was (1) higher than the average individual score and (2) higher than the best individual score. Groups should discuss the way in which individual members resolved disagreements and the effect of the ground rules on such behavior. They may consider the obstacles experienced in arriving at consensus agreements and the possible reasons for the difference between individual and group decisions.

Tally Sheet

Group Number	Group Score	Avg. Individual Score	Best Individual Score	Group Score Better Than Avg. Indiv.?	Group Score Better Than Best Indiv.?

Scoring Key: Question 3 is false; Question 6 is true; for all other questions the appropriate response is a question mark.

Comments on the exercise

Groups will nearly always perform better than the average individual on this exercise and will frequently perform better than the best individual in the group. When they do not, discussion with the group may indicate that a single individual imposed his decision on the group or that the group-process rules were violated. It should be emphasized in discussing this exercise that (1) groups are not always superior to individuals, but they often do better on this kind of judgmental task, and that (2) the use of the ground rules increases the likelihood of reaching consensus.

Worksheet

A businessman had just turned off the lights in the store when a man appeared and demanded money. The owner opened a cash register. The contents of the cash register were scooped up, and the man sped away. A member of the police force was notified promptly.

Statements about the story

1. A man appeared after the owner had turned off his store lights.   T   F   ?
2. The robber was a *man*.   T   F   ?
3. The man who appeared did not demand money.   T   F   ?
4. The man who opened the cash register was the owner.   T   F   ?
5. The store owner scooped up the contents of the cash register and ran away.   T   F   ?
6. Someone opened a cash register.   T   F   ?
7. After the man who demanded the money scooped up the contents of the cash register, he ran away.   T   F   ?
8. While the cash register contained money, the story does *not* state *how much*.   T   F   ?
9. The robber demanded money of the owner.   T   F   ?
10. The story concerns a series of events in which only three persons are referred to: the owner of the store, a man who demanded money, and a member of the police force.   T   F   ?
11. The following events in the story are true: someone demanded money, a cash register was opened, its contents were scooped up, and a man dashed out of the store.   T   F   ?

EXERCISE 2
CONDITIONS THAT LEAD TO CONFLICT
OR COOPERATION

The following exercise calls for individuals in the same organization to locate conflictive and cooperative conditions in any organization and then calls for them to identify those conditions which apply to their specific organization. The result of the exercise should be a greater intraorganizational dedication to cooperation.

Goal

To illustrate those conditions in an organization that contribute to conflict or to cooperation.

Group conditions

Two or more individuals who are members of the same organization.

Time required

About one hour.

Materials needed

Paper
Pencils
Flip chart, newsprint, or blackboard
Marker pens or chalk
Masking tape

Physical setting

Divide the larger group into pairs of subgroups. Each subgroup will have from one to five people.

Directions

Give each subgroup a sheet of newsprint and a marker pen. Tell the first subgroup in each pair that it is to make a list of conditions in any organization that maximize creativity, individuality, and trust. Tell the second subgroup in each pair to make a list of conditions in any organization that minimize trust and maximize dependency.

After about fifteen minutes bring each pair of subgroups together and ask them to post their lists, side by side, on the wall.

Tell all members in each group to read over all of the items listed by both subgroups and then to underline those statements that describe conditions which *presently* exist in their own organization. Each individual in each group should underline the conditions on the total list.

Discuss results.

Comments on the exercise

This exercise will identify many of the conditions discussed in Chapters 1 and 2 as contributing to conflict. In addition, it gives people a picture of their own organization in those terms. Threat and tension are minimized by depersonalizing the issues, since they are listed on sheets which do not identify the source and are a group product.

EXERCISE 3
INDIVIDUAL LEVELING AND FEEDBACK

This exercise (employing ideas developed in Chapter 3) is typical of those exercises used in sensitivity groups; it asks individuals to describe themselves and other members of the group and then calls for a feedback session to compare and contrast respective descriptions. The result of this exercise, of course, should be improved interpersonal relations.

Goal

To demonstrate the means for achieving common understanding about motives and behavior of individuals.

Group conditions

Two or more individuals.

Time required

Time varies directly with the size of the group; a group of five will take approximately one hour.

Materials needed

Pencils
Paper

Physical setting

Group members seated in circle.

Process

A. Each group member is asked to write the names of all group members, including himself, on a sheet of paper. Then, each member lists five adjectives that best describe each person listed.
B. When all group members have completed the first step, a volunteer is asked to listen to the adjectives describing him read by each of the other group members, with explanations if desired. Then, the volunteer will read his own list of five adjectives describing himself. All group members will then discuss discrepancies between self-perceptions and perceptions by other group members about the volunteer. When the first volunteer is finished, another person is asked to volunteer and this process continues until all members who wish to participate have done so.

Comments on the exercise

This exercise is helpful in demonstrating the different perceptions that individuals have about each other. The same method may be used to compare group perceptions about each other. The exercise will frequently stimulate discussion about the difference between self-perception and one's image to others. It will also serve as a confirming-action device for feedback when perceptions of a single individual are shared by the other group members.

EXERCISE 4
GIVING AND RECEIVING HELP
AND FEEDBACK

This exercise requires two individuals to help a third individual solve an interpersonal problem through respectively taking on the roles of consultant and observer. The exercise encourages the development of skills necessary for IDM. The results of the exercise should be exposure to problem definition and the search for solutions as well as increased feedback ability.

Goal

1. To gain skills in defining a problem and in helping another person deal with a problem.
2. To practice skills of feedback.
3. To identify Parent, Adult, and Child statements and the effect of such statements on interaction.

Group conditions

Any number of groups of three people.

Time required

One hour and fifteen minutes (three rounds with fifteen minutes for a discussion between the problem presenter and a consultant, followed by ten minutes for feedback by an observer).

Materials needed

One copy of Suggestions for Consultant in each group
One copy of Instructions for Presenter in each group
One copy of Suggestions for Observer in each group
One feedback worksheet for each group member
Pencils

Physical setting

Room which allows groups of three to sit comfortably together.

Process

A. Individuals are divided into groups of three. Materials are distributed so that each group has one set of role instructions and three copies of the feedback worksheet.
B. Group members are told that the purpose of the exercise is to get help on a real problem and to practice the skills of giving feedback and the use of the transactional analysis model.
  1. Group members are asked to decide who will be the problem presenter, the consultant, and the observer; then each reads the directions provided in the appropriate role instructions.
  2. Groups are told that they will have fifteen minutes for the discussion between the presenter and the consultant. During that time the observer will be silent.
  3. Then, the observer will have ten minutes to give feedback to both the presenter and the consultant about behavior that helped or hindered in the consultation process.
C. After twenty-five minutes, group members trade roles and proceed in the same way. After the second period has passed, the roles are again traded and the third period proceeds.
D. After the three periods are finished, all group members should assemble to discuss their experience.

Comments on the exercise

When using this exercise it is important for people to state a real problem that is felt personally. Otherwise, there is a tendency for people to intellectualize or to take refuge in abstraction. The trainer should remind people to describe rather than to judge; he should note the necessity of defining the problem and the value in separating problem definition from a search for solutions. It may be useful to post the rules for giving feedback and the language associated with Parent, Adult, and Child behavior for people to refer to during the exercise.

There will often be some frustration with the time constraints. The trainer may want to lengthen these at the outset to suit the type of group involved, but each round should be afforded equal time so that all group members have the same opportunity to practice the skills involved.

INSTRUCTIONS FOR THE PRESENTER

1. Your task is to consider, in detail, a problem which you are presently experiencing.

   Take a few minutes *now* to think about some specific problem you have which meets the following criteria:
   a. It is a problem in which *you* are directly involved.
   b. It is a problem which is presently *un*resolved.
   c. It is a problem that *you* want to do something about.
   d. It is a problem that is *interpersonal*—that is, it involves you and your relationship to another person or persons.
   e. It is a problem that is *important* to you.

   Please select a problem that exists in your relations with other people from your work, social, or family life, or one that exists because of the relationships *among* the groups of people with whom you relate. For example, the problem may exist because of the unique relationship between people with whom you work on the job and those with whom you interact on a social level.

2. Once you have selected the problem that is most critical for you, answer the following questions:
   a. What is the problem? Describe the problem in detail. Specify the nature of the problem, the people and the groups involved, their relationships with each other and with you, and the difficulties involved.
   b. Why do you think the problem exists? Describe the major events which led up to the problem and the reasons why the problem persists.
   c. How could you solve the problem? Describe the things you would like to do to solve the problem and the difficulties you see in implementing these changes. How would such changes affect you, the other person or persons involved, your relationships, and the groups involved?

SUGGESTIONS FOR THE CONSULTANT

1. Your task is to help the presenter define, or perhaps redefine, his problem and his relationship to it in sufficiently specific terms so that he may be able to take some steps toward solving it.

2. Questions to aid in problem definition:
   a. How does the presenter see himself in the situation? With sole personal responsibility? Enforcing authority? Developing motivation? Building group standards? Anything else?
   b. What seem to be fundamental difficulties? Who does what? What seems to happen? Why do they happen? What does not happen that would have been desirable? Any ideas about that?
   c. What solutions have been tried? With what results? What other solutions seem possible?
   d. Are there indications that others are concerned? Who? For what reasons? Who else might be concerned and for what reasons?
   e. Are there any indications from the presenter's behavior, as you know him, that he may not see some aspects of his own involvement in the problem? If so, can he do something about his part in the situation?

3. Cautions:
   a. Don't take over the problem. Resist the temptation to say such things as "The real problem seems to be . . ." or "You should do . . ." Instead, try, through the questions you ask, to help the presenter see things you may see.
   b. Don't disparage the problem. Resist the temptation to say such things as, "We had the same problem and solved it this way. It's not difficult." The problem is very real, and very unique to the presenter.

4. Guidelines:
   a. Focus particularly on questions such as: "Why?" "How do you know?" "What does this mean?"
   b. Try to help the presenter focus on what *he* can do—not on what *others* ought to do. We all have much more control over our own behavior than we do over the actions of other people.

SUGGESTIONS FOR THE OBSERVER

1. Your task is to observe and to listen to the presenter and the consultant as carefully as you can. Try to remain inconspicuous and to interfere as little as possible. When you make your remarks, comment briefly on what you saw taking place in such a way as to encourage the presenter and the consultant to think and talk about your observations.

2. Questions to ask yourself while observing:
   a. What is going on between the presenter and the consultant? Is one trying to influence the other? Trying to convince the other? Trying to talk down to the other? Are they listening to each other or talking around, across, or over each other?
   b. How does the consultant go about establishing a relationship? Do his remarks help the presenter speak freely?
   c. How carefully do the consultant and the presenter listen to each other? Do they seem to be really trying to understand the other person in the way that the other wishes to be understood?
   d. Do both presenter and consultant stay with defining and understanding the problem and the causes *before* trying to think of solutions?
   e. To what extent do presenter and consultant exhibit Parent, Adult, or Child language and behavior? What is the effect of such language or behavior on the other party?

3. Use the rules for feedback in making your report to the presenter and consultant.

FEEDBACK WORKSHEET FOR OBSERVER

What PRESENTER behavior . . .

helped to identify and to solve the problem?	hindered in the attempt to identify and to solve the problem?

What CONSULTANT behavior . . .

helped to identify and to solve the problem?	hindered in the attempt to identify and to solve the problem?

EXERCISE 5
INDIVIDUAL CHARACTERISTICS
AND OCCUPATION

In the following exercise, individuals are asked to select the occupations of three parties based on verbal portraits of them set forth by the author. The result of this exercise should be an increased sensitivity to the power and function of Parent images in everyday life.

Goal

To demonstrate Parent images shared by individuals.

Group conditions

Eight or more people.

Time required

Thirty minutes.

Physical setting

All individuals should be seated in one room.

Materials needed

Discussion guide for each person
Pencils
Flip chart, newsprint, or blackboard
Felt marker or chalk

Process

A. Distribute the discussion guide to all group members. Ask them to read the description of each of the three real people on the sheet and then to place A next to the one occupation at the bottom of the sheet that he or she feels Mr. A belongs to; B next to the one occupation that Ms. B belongs to; and C next to the one occupation that Mr. C belongs to.

B. While the group is completing the form, the trainer should write the predictions usually elicited by the exercise (see p. 157) on a sheet of paper.
C. When the group is finished, tally the number of votes for each occupation.
   1. Circle the occupation that received the most votes for A, B, and C.
   2. Then, display the sheet upon which the usual outcome is indicated.
   3. Discuss with the group the reason for similar outcomes on this exercise. It should be recalled that Parent roles contain stereotypes.
   4. Discuss the extent to which the descriptions of A, B, and C have anything to do with their ability to perform well in each of the occupations listed.
D. When the previous discussion is complete, reveal the actual occupations of the three people described. Discuss reactions.

Comments on the exercise

This exercise is useful in illustrating the stereotypes which we have in our Parent and how such images create judgments about people. Some individuals may engage in a discussion about how the facts described lead to only one obvious choice. In such instances it is useful to let the group explore how similar the people would be in any of the occupations stated, and how different they might be. If the group knows in detail about one occupation, they may explore factually how different or similar people are in that occupation and what stereotype is held about people in that occupation.

Discussion Guide

Personal characteristics

A. Mr. A was born into a wealthy Chicago family. He attended a private military academy during his high-school years and graduated from an eastern college.

During his adult years Mr. A has been considerably overweight, though his condition has not interfered with his occupation. He is an active member in several local service clubs and an avid card player. His trademark is a large black cigar upon which he is always puffing.

B. Ms. B is a statuesque and attractive woman in her early forties. She is prematurely gray and taller than most men. She attended a midwest college for four years followed by another period of specialized training.

During her vacations Ms. B likes to travel abroad, having made trips to Japan and Europe in the past. She is known by her associates to be a hard worker and skilled in dealing with people.

C. Mr. C is a quiet, soft-spoken gentleman in his late thirties. He is rather short with thinning blond hair and wears a hearing aid.

Mr. C is well liked by his associates. When not at work he spends his free time with his wife and two children.

He possesses a remarkable memory for numbers, being able to recall eight-digit numbers months after seeing them.

Occupation selection

From the list of occupations below, choose the one in which you feel each of the above persons belongs.

_____ Vice-President of manufacturing
_____ Nurse
_____ Army master sergeant
_____ Banker
_____ Long-haul truck driver
_____ Minister
_____ Accountant

Tally Sheet

	Number of Choices for:		
Occupation	Mr. A	Ms. B	Mr. C
Vice-President of manufacturing			
Nurse			
Army master sergeant			
Banker			
Truck driver			
Minister			
Accountant			

Prediction: Most people will say that Mr. A is either a vice-president of manufacturing or a banker, that Ms. B is a nurse, and that Mr. C is an accountant.

Actual: Mr. A is a Presbyterian minister in Loves Park, Illinois. Ms. B is a vice-president of manufacturing in a metal fabricating company in Madison, Wisconsin. Mr. C is an army master sergeant in a personnel office in Orleans, France. All are known by the author.

EXERCISE 6
THE PRISONER'S DILEMMA:
AN EXERCISE IN CONFLICT AND/OR
COOPERATION

In this exercise an individual group member is called upon to make decisions which will ultimately bear upon the positions of all the members of the group; the individual member has the option of competing or cooperating at strategic points in the exercise. The exercise demonstrates the advantages that accrue to individuals and groups who decide upon cooperation as a matter of policy.*

Goal

To demonstrate the effect of trust and other attitudes on problem-solving or competitive behavior.

Group conditions

Groups of four to twenty (divided into two subgroups).

Time required

A minimum of thirty minutes, often more nearly an hour.

* *This is a classic exercise with many variations. This version is based on the work of William Gellermann and adapted from J. Pfeiffer,* Structured Experiences for Human Relations Training, Vol. II, *Iowa City, Iowa: University Associates Press, 1970. Reprinted by permission of William Gellermann.*

Physical setting

Subgroups should be in separate rooms or with a physical divider between them; they should not be able to see or hear each other.

Materials needed

Tally sheet for each subgroup, either presented on a flip chart or printed for each member

Scoring directions for each subgroup, either presented on a flip chart or printed for each member

Pencils

Marker pens

Process

A. Groups are formed and divided into two subgroups. Instructions are given, a scorekeeper is assigned to each pair of subgroups, and subgroups move to their separate locations. Directions for scoring and tally sheets are placed at each location; they should be read by all members of the group.

B. After the instructions have been read, the following directions are given to all members:

1. The objective of this exercise is to earn as much as you can, without helping or hindering the other group. Each subgroup can make one of three choices in each of the ten rounds of the exercise: XX, XY, or YY. The scoring for each subgroup is based on the combined choice of both subgroups (see Scoring Sheet). In addition, the scoring for each round is cumulative. Rounds five, eight, and ten are bonus rounds with higher payoffs, and each subgroup will be given an opportunity before those rounds to send a representative to meet with a representative of the other subgroup, providing both groups wish to do so.

2. There are three key rules:
   a. The members of one subgroup are not to confer with the members of the other subgroup, except through a representative before rounds five, eight, and ten.
   b. Each subgroup must agree upon a single choice for each round.
   c. One subgroup is not to know the choice of the other subgroup until instructions are given to reveal it.

3. There are ten rounds to this exercise. During each round, subgroup members will have three minutes to determine their choice for the round. Remember the objective for this exercise (the exercise leader should write the objective on a flip chart so that it is visible to all subgroup members). Remember the rules.

4. After each round the scorekeeper collects the decision from each subgroup and conveys the total choice to each subgroup for scoring. One scorekeeper should be assigned to each pair of subgroups. He will need to keep the groups moving according to the time schedule.

5. Round five is a bonus round; you will note on the tally sheet that it is multiplied by three. Each subgroup will be asked by the scorekeeper before round three whether it wishes to send a representative to meet with a representative from the other subgroup. If both subgroups wish to have such a meeting, then they will be so informed by the scorekeeper and the two representatives will move to a separate location to engage in a discussion. The representatives will then return to the subgroups, and the subgroups will proceed to make their decisions as usual. The same procedure will be used before bonus rounds eight and ten.

6. Move to your subgroup location and make your decision for round one.

Comments on the exercise

After both subgroups have finished they should be brought back together for discussion. Key elements in the discussion should include:

1. Whether the "you" in the objective of the exercise refers to the subgroup or the total group.

2. How members interpreted the objective: for example, did they engage in win-lose competition?

3. How individual and group attitudes about the other group affected the behavior of the other group.

4. Whether subgroups instructed their representatives, if they chose to meet, or whether the subgroups merely placed representatives in such a position with no instructions: for example, did the members take responsibility for their representatives' actions?

5. Whether the subgroup or individual members of it were willing to adhere to their agreements with the other subgroup.

6. What form of leadership was exhibited in each subgroup and the effects of such leadership.

7. What effect communication between subgroups has upon cooperative or competitive behavior.

Scoring Instructions

For ten successive rounds each subgroup will choose XX, XY, or YY. The payoff for each round is dependent upon the combination of one subgroup's choice with the choice made by the other subgroup.

4 X's:	Lose $1.00 each
3 X's:	Win $1.00 each
1 Y :	Lose $3.00
2 X's:	Win $2.00 each
2 Y's:	Lose $2.00 each
1 X :	Win $3.00
3 Y's:	Lose $1.00 each
4 Y's:	Win $1.00 each

Tally Sheet

Round	Time Allowed	Subgroup A			Subgroup B		
		Subgroup A Choice	Gain or Loss	Cumulative Total	Subgroup B Choice	Gain or Loss	Cumulative Total
1	3 min.						
2	3 min.						
3	3 min.						
4	3 min.						
Bonus Round: Payoff multiplied by 3 — 5	5 min. for meeting + 3 min.						
6	3 min.						
7	3 min.						
Bonus Round: Payoff multiplied by 5 — 8	5 min. for meeting + 3 min.						
9	3 min.						
Bonus Round: Payoff multiplied by 10 — 10	5 min. for meeting + 3 min.						

EXERCISE 7
THE CHANGE OF WORK PROCEDURE

This exercise places individuals in a problem-solving situation concerning a hypothetical work procedure where they can employ choice behavior or integrative decision making. The result of the exercise should be a positive practical experience with IDM which can, in turn, contribute to successful application of the method in real-life situations.*

Goal

To demonstrate the difference between choice behavior and integrative decision making.

Group conditions

Requires, at minimum, two groups of four, not counting observers. Best used with four or more groups of five, including an observer in each group.

Time required

Thirty minutes for role playing and thirty minutes for preparation and reporting.

Materials needed

General instructions for each member
One role instruction for each member
3" × 5" cards
Masking tape
Flip chart, newsprint, or blackboard
Marker pens or chalk

---

* *From* Supervisory and Executive Development *by N. R. F. Maier, A. Solem, and A. A. Maier. Copyright © 1957 by John Wiley & Sons, Inc. Reprinted by permission of Norman R. F. Maier. In the following material, the "Process" and "Implications" sections are quoted directly.*

Process

A. Preparation
1. The audience should divide themselves into groups of four. Those left over after groups have been formed may join separate groups to participate as observers. Their instructions are on page 171.
2. All groups are to select one of their members to act as the foreman, Gus Thompson. After the foremen have been chosen they should raise their hands to indicate that the group has a conference leader.
3. The other three individuals in each group will be crew members. Beginning with the foreman and going in clockwise order, their names will be Jack, Steve, and Walt.
4. When all members have received their roles, the trainer should read aloud the section entitled General Information.
5. The role-players should then study their individual roles in preparation for the small-group discussions. The role for Gus Thompson is on page 167; that for Jack is on page 168; Steve's role is on page 169; and Walt's is on page 170. Participants should read only their own roles.
6. The Gus Thompsons should stand up beside their groups when they have finished studying their roles, thus giving the instructor a signal that they are ready to begin.

B. Process
1. When all foremen are standing, the instructor may help to set the stage for the role playing by commenting that the foreman has asked the crew members to meet with him in his office to discuss a problem before starting work. He should explain that when the foreman is asked to sit down this will be the signal that Gus has entered his office. He hopes that the men will speak to him as he enters.
2. When everyone understands his function, the trainer should ask the foremen to sit down. All groups should role-play simultaneously.
3. During the role-playing the exercise leader should prepare a blackboard with the headings shown in Sample Table, page 172. This table is to be used for recording the results of the various group discussions.
4. Approximately 25 minutes are needed by the average group to reach a decision. At the end of this period the trainer should observe the process of the various groups. If most of them have finished he should give the remaining few groups a two-minute warning signal.

C. Collecting Results
1. The foreman of each group should report the solution agreed upon. The trainer should enter the solution, in abbreviated form, in the proper column of the table he has prepared (see Sample Table).

Care should be taken to include any special or unique features such as rest pauses, partial rotation procedures, arrangements for helping one another, etc.

2. The foreman should indicate the degree of his satisfaction with the solution so that the instructor can enter his response in Column 2.

3. The members in each crew should indicate whether they are satisfied or dissatisfied with the results. The trainer should indicate the number satisfied in Column 3. Occasionally a member will be mildly inclined in one direction or the other, in which case a question mark should be entered to indicate his feelings.

4. Each foreman is asked whether any crew members were unusually stubborn, hostile, or troublesome and, if so, who these were. Then the initials of the members should be written in Column 4 of the table.

5. The crew members should report whether they think production will go up, down, or remain the same as the result of the discussion. When they think there will be a change, they should agree on a percent increase or decrease, and the trainer should enter this figure in Column 5 of the table.

6. The observers (or crew members) should report what they feel is the main thing the leader did to help the group reach their decision. The members should agree on this point so that the trainer can summarize their consensus on the blackboard under Column 6.

7. The observers (or crew members) should report what the leader did to hinder the discussion the most. This point should be summarized on the blackboard under Column 7.

D. Classification of Solutions

1. After the results from all groups have been tabulated, the solutions should be reviewed briefly in a general group discussion to determine which solutions represent rejection of changes in work method. These can be indicated by the letter R in the margin.

2. Solutions that indicate acceptance of the management solution with minor or no modifications should be selected by the group and labeled with the letter A in the margin.

3. The remaining solutions should be examined for new features and various compromises, such as rest pauses, partial rotation, more time in best position, ways for the crew to help one another, trial periods, and so on. These solutions should be indicated in the margin by the letter C. They represent compromises and the development of new ideas. A short time may be taken to discuss the contributions of the various types of provisions to the satisfaction of the crew members.

4. The solutions should be examined to determine the numbers which are provisional or for a limited trial period. Some time should be spent to discuss why foremen made these concessions.

E. Evaluation of Methods Used
1. The attitudes of the leaders should be discussed in relation to the types of solutions developed. General conclusions should be drawn as to what constitutes a helpful leader attitude versus an obstructive attitude.
2. Discussion should be used to determine the ways in which the airing of feelings and hostilities in the crew influenced the final outcome.
3. On the basis of the tabulated results and the role-playing experience, the group should attempt to determine the foreman's part in influencing the outcome of the discussion. Both satisfaction and productivity should be considered in relation to the type of solution reached and to the foreman's conduct, as described in Columns 6 and 7.
4. Column 4 should be examined to determine whether certain crew members caused most of the trouble. If different men were troublemakers in the various groups, this suggests that certain events in the discussion, rather than the role instructions, were the cause of their troublesome behavior. In any case, the problem employees should report why they acted as they did.

F. Analysis of Resistance Forces
1. From the group as a whole, the instructor should obtain the various objections to change expressed by the different crew members and list these on the blackboard. This list usually will include such factors as aversion to boredom, dislike of the time-study man, fear of rate cuts, fear of speed-up, fear of running out of work, and the like.
2. Next to the objections the trainer should develop a list of the possible gains or advantages to the crew by changing to the new method. Usually the item of more pay will be mentioned. Other factors, such as time for rest pauses, satisfaction with being in one's best position, etc., may be offered. However, only those aspects actually mentioned in the role-playing discussion should be accepted.
3. The two sets of items listed as (a) objections to changing work methods and (b) advantages of change can now be considered as forces against change and forces toward change, respectively.
4. The list of resistances to the new work method can now be examined in discussion to determine the ones that indicate fear and hostility and those that have a more intellectual basis.
5. Ways for reducing fears and negative feelings should be discussed.
6. Methods for dealing with realistic objections to change, for example, the boredom problem, should be discussed.
7. Evaluation of employee participation methods for obtaining acceptance of change should be discussed in relation to methods which do not involve participation of employees in making changes. Em-

phasis should be given to a comparison of the motivational effects of participation vs. nonparticipation.

8. The relative importance of solution quality vs. acceptance should be discussed. Is the most efficient solution without acceptance preferable to a less efficient solution having acceptance?

Role Instructions

GENERAL INFORMATION

In a company manufacturing subassemblies for the automobile industry, the assembly work is done by small groups of employees. Several of these groups are under the supervision of a foreman, Gus Thompson. In one of these groups, Jack, Steve, and Walt work together assembling fuel pumps.

This operation is divided into three jobs or positions, called Position 1, Position 2, and Position 3. Supplies for each position are located next to the bench where the man works. The men work side by side and can help each other out if they wish. Since all the jobs are simple and fairly similar these three employees exchange positions on the line every now and then. This trading of positions was developed by the men themselves. It creates no financial problem because the crew is paid by a group piece rate. In this way the three members share the production pay equally.

ROLE FOR GUS THOMPSON, FOREMAN

You are the foreman in a shop and supervise the work of about 20 men. Most of the jobs are piece rate jobs and some of the men work in teams and are paid on a team piece rate basis. In one of the teams, Jack, Walt, and Steve work together. Each one of them does one of the operations for an hour and then they exchange, so that all men perform each of the operations at different times. The men themselves decided to operate that way and you have never given the plan any thought.

Lately, Jim Clark, the methods man, has been around and studied conditions in your shop. He timed Jack, Walt, and Steve on each of the operations and came up with the following facts.

TIME PER OPERATION (IN MINUTES)

	Position 1	Position 2	Position 3	Total
Jack	3	4	4½	11½
Walt	3½	3½	3	10
Steve	5	3½	4½	13
				34½

He observed that with the men rotating, the average time for all three operations would be ⅓ of the total time or 11½ minutes per complete unit. If, however, Jack worked in the number 1 spot, Steve in the number 2 spot, and Walt in the number 3 spot, the time would be 9½ minutes, a reduction of over 17%. Such a reduction in time would amount to a saving of more than 80 minutes. In other words the lost production is about the same as that which would occur if the men loafed for 80 minutes in an 8-hour day. If the time were used for productive effort, production would be increased more than 20%.

This made pretty good sense to you so you have decided to take up the problem with the men. You feel that they should go along with any change in operation that is made.

ROLE FOR JACK

You are one of three men on an assembly operation. Walt and Steve are your teammates and you enjoy working with them. You get paid on a team basis and you are making wages that are entirely satisfactory. Steve isn't quite as fast as Walt and you, but when you feel he is holding things up too much each of you can help out.

The work is very monotonous. The saving thing about it is that every hour you all change positions. In this way you get to do all three operations. You are best on the number 1 position so when you get in that spot you turn out some extra work and so make the job easier for Steve who follows you in that position.

You have been on this job for two years and have never run out of work. Apparently your group can make pretty good pay without running yourselves out of a job. Lately, however, the company has had some of its experts hanging around. It looks like the company is trying to work out some speed-up methods. If they make these jobs any more simple you won't be able to stand the monotony. Gus Thompson, your foreman, is a decent guy and has never criticized your team's work.

ROLE FOR STEVE

You work with Jack and Walt on an assembly job and get paid on a team piece rate basis. The three of you work very well together and make a pretty good wage. Jack and Walt like to make a little more than you think is necessary, but you go along with them and work as hard as you can so as to keep the production up where they want it. They are good fellows and often help you out if you fall behind, so you feel it is only fair to try and go along with the pace they set.

The three of you exchange positions every hour. In this way you get to work all positions. You like the number 2 position the best because it is easiest. When you get in the number 3 position you can't keep up and then feel Gus Thompson, the foreman, watching you. Sometimes Walt and Jack slow down when you are on the number 3 spot and then the foreman seems satisfied.

Lately the methods man has been hanging around watching the the job. You wonder what he is up to. Can't they leave guys alone who are doing all right?

ROLE FOR WALT

You work with Jack and Steve on a job that requires three separate operations. Each of you works on each of the three operations by rotating positions once every hour. This makes the work more interesting and you can always help out the other fellow by running the job ahead in case one of you doesn't feel so good. It's all right to help out because you get paid on a team piece rate basis. You could actually earn more if Steve were a faster worker, but he is a swell guy and you would rather have him in the group than someone else who might do a little bit more.

You find all three positions about equally desirable. They are all simple and purely routine. The monotony doesn't bother you much because you can talk, daydream, and change your pace. By working slow for a while and then fast you can sort of set your pace to music you hum to yourself. Jack and Steve like the idea of changing jobs and even though Steve is slow on some positions, the changing around has its good points. You feel you get to a stopping place every time you change positions and this kind of takes the place of a rest pause.

Lately some kind of efficiency expert has been hanging around. He stands some distance away with a stopwatch in his hand. The company could get more for its money if it put some of those guys to work. You say to yourself, "I'd like to see one of these guys try and tell me how to do this job. I'd sure give him an earful."

If Gus Thompson, your foreman, doesn't get him out of the shop pretty soon, you're going to tell him what you think of his dragging in company spies.

INSTRUCTIONS FOR OBSERVERS

1. Observe the leader's attitude toward change during the discussion.
   A. Was he partial to the new method?
   B. Did he seem mainly interested in more production or in improving the job for the crew?
   C. To what extent was he considerate of the objections raised by the crew? How did he react to their opposition?
   D. Did he defend the new method or argue for its acceptance? What effect did this have on progress in this discussion?
2. Make notes on characteristic aspects of the discussion.
   A. Did arguments develop?
   B. Was any crew member unusually stubborn?
   C. Did the crew members have their say?
   D. Did the leader really listen?
   E. What were the main points of differences?
3. Observe evidences of problem-solving behavior.
   A. What was agreed upon, if anything?
   B. In what respects was there a willingness to problem solve?
   C. What did the leader do to help or hinder a mutually acceptable work method?

SAMPLE TABLE—GROUP RESULTS ON PROPOSED CHANGE

(Use Table for Recording Data)

Group No.	1 Solution	2 Foreman satisfied	3 Number satisfied in crew	4 Problem employees	5 Future production	6 Leader actions that helped	7 Leader actions that hindered

Implications

The solutions obtained by various groups usually fall into two categories: those in which the old rotation method will be continued, sometimes with the group's promise that they will try to increase production if allowed to continue the old method; and those in which the men accept the plan suggested by the time-study man, usually with the understanding that they can return to the old method if they wish. The foreman ordinarily goes along with either decision, indicating that he either convinces the group that they should change or the group convinces him that they should not change. Most foremen recognize the importance of gaining acceptance and invariably they make the concession of allowing the change to be on a trial basis. The men know they can make or break a solution with this provision. Thus, regardless of the outcome, a discussion tends to bring about a meeting of minds.

Now and then the conflict will not be resolved and then there is dissatisfaction. Often the men threaten a walkout if the foreman goes ahead with the change or threatens to discharge individuals who refuse to make the change.

The reason why solutions tend to fall into two categories is partially due to the way the problem is posed. When the foreman suggests a plan, the men can either accept it or reject it. Thus the problem becomes a choice between the new and the old way.

However, if the foreman does not suggest a new method but presents the facts obtained by the time-study man and indicates that the men can use the facts in any way they see fit, no one solution is favored by the foreman. As a result, a variety of solutions is possible, each of which not only takes the time-study facts into account but also makes use of the feelings of the men toward their jobs. Examples of such solutions are (a) Jack and Walt exchange jobs, but Steve works permanently at his best position; (b) each man alternates between his two best positions; and (c) the old rotation plan is continued, but each man works a longer stretch on his best position.

An experimental study made with this case [*] demonstrated that the selling approach resulted in none of the above three types of solutions, whereas the problem-solving approach yielded 37.5 percent of such solutions. These solutions replaced nearly all of the resistance-to-change solutions that the selling approach yielded in 50 percent of the groups.

When groups participate in change, resistance is greatly reduced [**]

[*] N. R. F. Maier, "An Experimental Test of the Effect of Training on Discussion Leadership," Human Relations, 1953, 6, 161–73.
[**] L. Coch and J. R. P. French, Jr., "Overcoming Resistance to Change," Human Relations, 1948, 1, 512–532.

because people do not have to fear decisions they make themselves. This means that consultative management does not go far enough toward participation, since involvement that merely allows the voicing of objections falls short of involvement in the solution. However, the consultative approach is better than the selling method because too skillful a selling technique may actually increase fear. Of course, the direct approach of enforcing a change because it is management's prerogative engenders the most fear and hostility.

In handling a discussion in a problem of this sort it is desirable to differentiate between various forms of resistance. In this particular case it is probable that the following types of response were supplied as reasons for not changing:

A. Hostility toward the time-study man.
B. Claims of boredom from working on one position.
C. Fear of piecerate cuts.
D. Distrust of management's motives.

These four types of response may be divided into two categories: emotional, and factual or situational. All except the statements about boredom involve attitudes and emotion. To a great extent these may be imagined or unfounded, but regardless of how unreal they may be, they are a source of feeling. This means that they are not subject to change through reason and logical refutation.

Responses having an emotional loading must be expressed by the group and accepted by the leader. He can use such phrases as, "I can see that the time-study man bothered you"; "Do the rest of you feel the same way?" "I am sorry if I didn't explain his function to you." The leader can give the group confidence and assurance by such statements as "You understand we don't have to use the time-study man's data" or "An expert's job is to supply information, but we will decide what to do with it." The release of emotional expression, acceptance of feelings, and assurance of status reduce emotional responses, while arguments and facts increase them because they threaten. The discussion leader's attitude, understanding, and tolerance will also aid him in being patient and willing to listen, even to unreasonable statements.

When various hostilities and fears have been expressed, the group will become interested in facts. They will ask questions and may supply facts of their own. This is the beginning of problem solving.

The objection of boredom may now be seriously considered by the leader. The men may have mentioned it in connection with the other emotional responses, but now it remains as a true obstacle. They see a change as boring and in a sense they are in a rut, since for them change is synonymous with each man working his best position. When thinking seems to be curtailed by a lack of variety, the leader can do a lot to break up this stereotypy in thought. He can ask, "Are there any ways of relieving bore-dom other than by our present method of rotating?" This question tends to separate the old method as a way of doing the job from its merits for deal-ing with monotony. Once working the old way is no longer associated with absence of boredom, and a change as leading to boredom, it becomes pos-sible to search for a new method that is not boring. Thus the above ques-tion causes the men to think of rest pauses, music, partial rotation, and modified rotation as aspects of new methods.

The use of exploratory questions is an excellent leadership approach for dealing with sterility in thinking because a group often finds itself in a rut as far as ideas are concerned. It is a device for improving the quality of group thinking, once emotional resistance has been reduced. However, it is not recommended when the group is angry or defensive, since the leader must not influence the direction of thinking on such occasions. Exploratory questions do not direct a group toward certain ideas, but they cause the group to look elsewhere; and as long as variability is stimulated, progress in ideas can be made.

Comments on the exercise *

This exercise illustrates the difference between choice behavior (focusing upon the old work procedure or the new work procedure) and integrative decision making, (turning choices into problems and then search-ing for alternatives which satisfy stated objectives), as well as illustrating the effect of space, perceptions, attitudes, and language on the ability to achieve such an integrative decision.

When choice behavior is used, the group will often divide itself spatially so that Gus is facing Steve, Walt, and Jack. The discussion will center on persuasion and argument about Gus' method versus the workers' method. In such cases, Gus will rarely share the facts regarding detailed times at each work station. This behavior will generally result in a win-lose or a lose-lose outcome.

When integrative methods are used, the discussion at some point will shift to an identification of needs or objectives. The workers may say that they want more money, a work method that is not boring, and a solu-tion that will keep Gus happy and the team together. Gus may say that he wants increased productivity, a satisfied work group, and a satisfactory solution to report to his boss. A typical statement of the problem for every-one may be as follows: "What methods can we find which will increase production, avoid boredom, keep the team together, and satisfy Gus and the workers?"

* By A. C. Filley.

Since the problem depends on strong elements of both solution quality and solution acceptability, it should become clear that the best solution on paper, the new work procedure, will not in fact generate the most production if it is not acceptable to the workers. If all members attack the problem and follow the principles for integrative methods, including the use of Adult language, they will frequently derive an integrative solution.

The trainer should take care to see that at least some groups achieve an integrative solution. If it is clear that all groups are fixed on a choice method, then the trainer may wish to intervene in one or more groups to help them identify the problems. By having some groups achieve win-lose or lose-lose methods while others achieve win-win methods, the contrast between the respective outcomes may be emphasized, and the ability to use integrative methods may be demonstrated. It is far more persuasive for participants to see their peers using the problem-solving method and deriving an integrative solution than it is for a trainer to talk about the method and illustrate theoretical solutions.

Index